IMAGES OF ENGLAND

THE PRISON SERVICE IN BRITAIN

IMAGES OF ENGLAND

THE PRISON SERVICE IN BRITAIN

BEVERLEY BAKER AND LAURA BUTLER

TEMPUS

First published 2006

Tempus Publishing Limited
The Mill, Brimscombe Port,
Stroud, Gloucestershire, GL5 2QG
www.tempus-publishing.com

British Library Cataloguing in Publication Data.
A catalogue record for this book is available from the British Library.

ISBN 0 7524 4190 6

Typesetting and origination by Tempus Publishing Limited.
Printed in Great Britain.

Contents

Introduction

Prisons, until the eighteenth century, usually occupied space within other secure buildings such as a county town castle, bridge or civic building. They were primarily places to hold prisoners awaiting trial or punishment, including execution, corporal punishment, transportation or fines. As holding prisons standards were poor, until John Howard, the renowned prison reformer, paved the way for change in prisons in the eighteenth century. His assessment of prisons in Britain and Europe led to the introduction of two significant Acts of Parliament which attempted to improve conditions for prisoners and abolish the requirement for prisoners to pay a discharge fee at the end of their sentences. The 1779 Penitentiary Act, for example, had a profound impact on the development of prisons, introducing separated sleeping cells and limited association between prisoners.

The nineteenth century saw a number of further developments in the prison system. The 1823 Gaol Act was the first of many which sought to impose standards and uniformity in the administration and management of local prisons. In search of a new design for prisons and a means of improving control over the inmates, inspiration was sought from America in the form of the silent system where prisoners served their sentences in total silence, and the separate system in which prisoners were held in solitary confinement for twenty-three hours a day, only relieved by an hour's exercise. The separate system was recommended in the 1835 report of a committee of the House of Lords and in 1842 Pentonville was the first institution designed specifically for the adoption of the separate system. By 1850 around sixty British prisons had been rebuilt or were being altered to conform to the separate system. This strict regime was not just restricted to the cells but also extended to the exercise yards and chapels.

In 1877 the Prison Act transferred the responsibility for managing and financing prisons in Britain from the local justices to the Home Secretary. In addition, a new body, the Prison Commission, was established to take on the administrative responsibility for the prison system. This was the beginning of a national prison system. The first chairman of the Prison Commission was Sir Edmund du Cane who was responsible for organising and enforcing an efficient and uniformed prison system. Du Cane's prison regime adopted the separate system alongside unproductive hard work done in solitary confinement for the first month of a prisoner's sentence and then in association under strict silence.

However by the end of the nineteenth century, confidence in the separate system as an effective means of controlling prisoners came under question. The Gladstone Committee in 1895 recommended that the prison's primary functions should be deterrence and reform rather than punishment. The committee suggested that unproductive work, such as the crank and treadwheel, should be abolished, and that productive work in association, as carried out in convict prisons, should be extended to all local prisons. The committee recommended numerous other changes, including further classification of prisoners, wider availability of books, and the extension of educational facilities, which were to form the basis of a programme of improvements throughout the first half of the twentieth century.

The twentieth century saw the dawn of the borstal system with the establishment of the first borstal in 1908 on the site of Rochester convict prison. These institutions were created for the detention and reform of young offenders.

The inter-war period was to be marked by the appointment of Alexander Paterson to the Prison Commission. He was the driving force behind many of the recommendations implemented by the Commissioners which included abolishment of the broad arrow uniform, the relaxation of the silent rule, the introduction of a seven hour working day and payment of a wage for the work undertaken by prisoners.

Further developments took place after the Second World War with the introduction of detention and remand centres and the establishment of the Central After-Care Association responsible for the after-care of released prisoners. 1947 saw the expansion of educational facilities provided by local education authorities inside prisons. Home leave, which had been a privilege used in borstals, was introduced to adult prisons in 1951.

The 1960s saw the development of further professionalism in, and support for, prison staff with the opening of a second Officer Training School at HMP Leyhill in 1962 and the establishment of the Working Party on the Role of the Prison Officer, which examined the contribution that officers could make to the improvement of prison regimes. The Prison Commission was replaced by the Prison Department of the Home Office in 1963. More specialised prisons were also introduced during this decade including Grendon prison, established for the psychiatric treatment of offenders, and Coldingley prison, designed for a predominantly industrial regime. However, the 1960s were also overshadowed by several high profile escapes which led to the Mounbatten Inquiry, which examined security within prisons. Although various recommendations were implemented to improve security within prisons, such as the introduction of CCTV and a new classification system for adult male prisoners, continuing overcrowding and financial constraints still put pressure on the prison service. This culminated in a number of serious disturbances during 1990 in over twenty prisons around the country, leading to the commission of the Woolfe Inquiry into the state of British prisons.

Prisons have, over the centuries, gone through periods of acute change and development, with constant questioning of their role, structure and governance – therefore what lies ahead for our prisons in the twenty-first century?

Glossary

After-care – Training and assistance given to prisoners towards the end of their sentence and after release to help the offender reintegrate back into society.

Borstal – An institution used to detain offenders aged between sixteen and twenty-one years old, with the aim of reformation through a system based on English public schools. They were introduced in 1902.

Bridewell – An institution with the purpose of punishing and enforcing work upon the homeless and idle.

Convicted Prisoner – A person in prison who has been convicted of the crime they have been charged with.

Detention Centre – An institution used to detain offenders aged between fourteen and twenty-one years old who are serving short sentences. The emphasis is on discipline.

Gibbet – The made-to-measure metal frame in which a criminal's corpse would sometimes be publicly displayed after they had been hung, to deter others from committing crimes. Abolished in 1832.

Hard Labour – Physically demanding work specified as part of the sentence given by the courts.

House of Correction – See Bridewell.

Industrial School – An institution where children under the age of fourteen who were either homeless, caught begging or whose parents found them uncontrollable were detained. They were taught the elementary subjects as well as an industry.

Juvenile Centre – An institution to hold offenders aged between fifteen and seventeen years old.

Juvenile Offender – Offenders aged between fifteen and seventeen years old.

Open Prison – Minimum security institutions that hold prisoners of the lowest security category.

Penitentiary – An institution where prisoners were kept in solitary confinement and had to carry out hard labour.

Prison Welfare Officers – Probation Officers stationed in prisons who help prepare inmates for release, often through referral to outside agencies. Introduced in 1955.

Probation Service – The body that governs the supervision of offenders released into the community on the condition of good behaviour in substitution of part or a full prison sentence. Established in 1907.

Reformatory School – An institution to which offenders under the age of sixteen are sent to be reformed, which was also be used alongside a term of imprisonment.

Release on License/ Parole - The term used to describe when convicted prisoners are released from prison earlier than the end of the term of their sentence on the condition of good behaviour. They would be supervised by a member of the Probation Service. Introduced in 1968.

Remand Centre – An institution where prisoners awaiting trial were detained.

Remand Prisoner – Those who are awaiting trial but who have been refused bail by the courts.

Segregation Unit – A group of cells separate from the normal living cells that have minimal furniture and are used as a punishment or to protect the inmate (from themselves or others).

Separate System – A method of prison management formed around the idea of prisoners being kept in isolation from each other. Introduced in 1839

Short, Sharp, Shock System – A regime practiced in the 1970s that tried to reduce recidivism in young offenders by brief harsh spells of incarceration.

Silent System – A method of prison management with silence being enforced at all times.

Slopping out – The act of emptying the chamber pots in the morning after a night's confinement in the cells.

Solitary Confinement – Removing a prisoner from the company of other people.

Useless Labour – A form of hard labour that has no productive conclusion. It is also known as unproductive labour. Abolished in 1899.

Young Offender – An offender aged between eighteen and twenty-one years old.

Youth Custody Centre – Now known as Young Offender Institutes. These are institutions where offenders aged between eighteen and twenty-one years old are detained.

Acknowledgements

The photographs included in this book form part of the HM Prison Service Collection held at the NCCL Galleries of Justice Museum, based in the old Shire Hall, in the historic Lace Market area of Nottingham city centre. The Shire Hall consists of two grand Victorian courtrooms, the County Gaol with its medieval cells, and the County Police Headquarters. The museum's displays chart the history of imprisonment and the development of the HM Prison Service over the centuries, as well as the history of policing in Britain. The museum's archive collection dates from the 1500s, and covers every aspect of the British Criminal Justice system, from policing, trials and prisons, to probation. It contains prison registers, governor's and Chaplain's journals, trial papers, letters, photographs, and so provides a unique insight into the history of criminal justice. Access to the archive and library can be made via an appointment.

The NCCL Galleries of Justice is an independent museum and educational charity.

Tel: 0115 952 0555
Email: info@nccl.org.uk
Website: www.nccl.org.uk

Beverley Baker has been the Librarian/Archivist of the museum since 1999 and has recently taken up the post of Collections Manager.

Laura Butler is a criminology graduate and research volunteer for the museum.

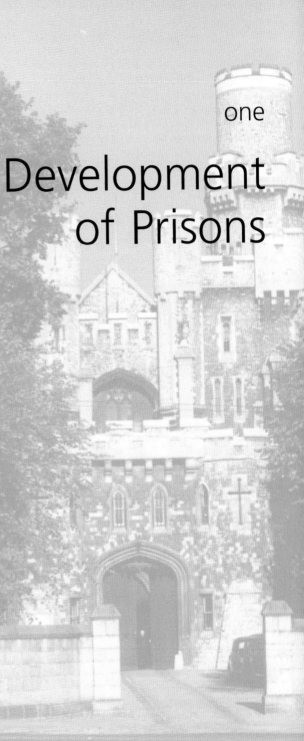

one

Development
of Prisons

Left: Four medieval prison cells at HM Prison Jersey. Local prisons were the oldest form of prison establishments dating as far back as Saxon times. They consisted of two types: gaols and houses of correction. In medieval and early modern times the gaols were primarily used for the detention of criminals and for the punishment of those who had done wrong. By the fifteenth century gaols were used to hold debtors in private disputes until they had paid their dues. In the eighteenth century the largest proportion of those in gaol were debtors. During his tour of prisons in the 1770s, the prison reformer John Howard assessed that out of the 4,084 prisoners, 2,437 were debtors.

Below: Castle Rushen, Castletown, Isle of Man. Built around 945 by Guthred the Dane, this medieval castle housed the courthouse and the gibbet. The castle's keep with its dark and dismal cells was used for the confinement of prisoners. In 1663, eight Quakers were imprisoned for their absence from public worship, confined in the high tower without fire or candles during the cold winter season for fifteen weeks. In 1765, three additional rooms were allocated for the imprisonment of debtors and criminals. The castle underwent some remodelling in 1815 in order to improve the accommodation for prisoners and the confinement of lunatics. After years of condemnation, the castle ceased to be used as a prison in 1891.

Castle Rushen.

Right: HM Prison Lancaster Castle consists of an extensive group of historic buildings, including: the twelfth-century keep; the fourteenth-century well tower (also known as the witches' tower); the fifteenth-century gatehouse, named after John O'Gaunt (the Duke of Lancaster 1359); and the nineteenth-century female penitentiary. More death sentences were handed down at Lancaster Castle than any other court in England, except Newgate. It was one of the first gaols in England to segregate female and child prisoners from their male counterparts. It is still used today as both a court and a prison and is considered to be the oldest serving prison in Europe.

Below: HM Prison Gloucester (*c.* 1900) was considered the most influential of the new local prisons built during the 1780s. It was inspired by Sir George Onesiphorous Paul, the High Sheriff of Gloucester who was also responsible for reforming the county's prison system with the building of a County Gaol and the five Bridewells. Built between 1785 and 1789 and opened in 1791, it imposed 'solitary confinement', a psychological form of discipline that was set out in the Penitentiary Act 1779. It was thought that solitary confinement would stop the spread of both gaol fever and immorality amongst the prisoners.

The debtors' prison in HM Prison Gloucester was built in 1826 to hold forty male debtors and four female debtors. It was built on a triangular plot of land to the east of the prison site, a two-storey brick building which contained cells on the first floor and open rooms on the ground floor.

HM Prison Jersey, the debtors' house within the walls of the prison, 1960. Prior to the mid-nineteenth century, debtors' prisons were a common way to deal with unpaid debt. The Debtors Act 1869 abolished imprisonment for debt, although debtors who had the means to pay their debt, but did not do so, could still be imprisoned for up to six weeks.

HM Prison Holloway. The original prison was built in 1852 at a cost of £91,547 and accommodated 350 prisoners. It has been described as a noble building of the castellated style, the battlements and lofty tower being reminiscent of a castle. It had three wings for males, containing a total of 436 cells, and one wing for females and juveniles, with a total of sixty cells for females and sixty-two for juveniles. Due to the closure of Newgate Prison in 1901 there was a need for more places for female prisoners. Therefore, in 1903 Holloway was refurbished into a solely female prison with a capacity for 949 female prisoners.

HM Prison Holloway, 1983. The old prison was slowly replaced by a new prison built on the same site. Work started in 1970 and was completed in 1984 at an estimated cost of £40 million. Holloway is now an all-purpose women's prison, serving the southern half of England. Its population includes remand and trial prisoners, convicted prisoners serving short, medium and long sentences, Youth Custody Centre trainees and highly disturbed psychiatric cases from all over the country.

Left: The griffin (Gryphon) is a mythical creature often found in heraldry. The porch of the original HM Prison Holloway had a pillar either side, each surmounted by a large winged griffin. One of the griffins clasped a set of leg irons; the other held a key in one of his talons and a large leg iron in the other. Fortunately these original griffins were preserved during the rebuilding of Holloway and now flank the entrance to the new prison.

Below: HM Prison Bedford. In 1900 a small group of offenders from London were carefully selected according to their potential to respond to specialised training. They were taken to Bedford Prison where they were taught a trade and helped to start a new life upon discharge from prison. This was the beginning of what was to become known as the Borstal System. The first borstals occupied existing institutions: Rochester Convict Prison in Kent; Portland Convict Prison; and Feltham Industrial School. The first female borstal was established in the former State Inebriate Reformatory inside Aylesbury's women's prison on 30 August 1909.

Opposite below: Borstal boys' room in the new block at HM Borstal Institution Dover, 1974. Dover Borstal was situated on Western Heights which has been a fortified area since the Roman times. In 1952 the Prison Commission took over the site from the Army, converting it into a medium security prison for corrective detainees. By 1957 it operated as a borstal and continued to hold young offenders until 2002 when it was re-designated as an Immigration Removal Centre.

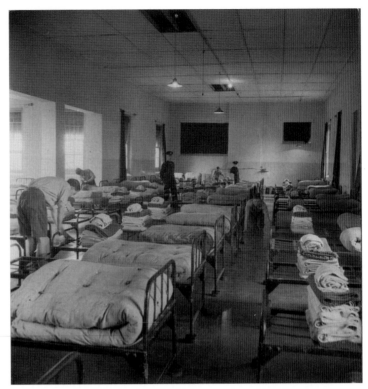

Right: HM Prison and Borstal Institution Feltham was the second borstal to be established and opened in 1911 to cater for the rise in committals. In 1920 a 'reception class' was established so that a 'mental diagnosis' could be made in order to separate out cases of unstable mentality as well as an attempt to assess the young offenders' general capacity for education and training. All boys slept in dormitories.

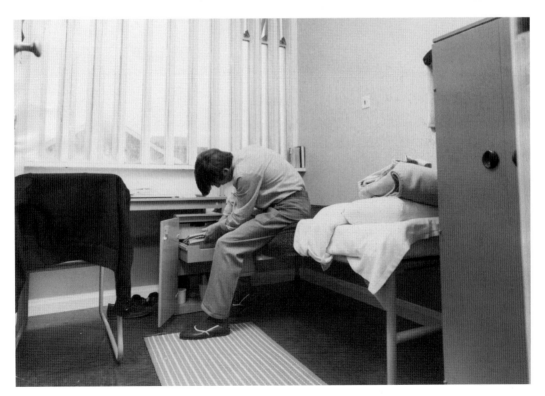

Interior of a cell at HM Prison Wakefield in the 1940s. Wakefield Prison was influential in the development of the prison system during the nineteenth and twentieth centuries. In 1834 it was one of the first to introduce the silent system. After the Local Justices responsible for the running of Wakefield Prison visited Ireland to observe the 'Irish System' used in their prisons, they introduced a similar system of reward. Promotion was determined by the number of marks earned for good conduct. The top class of promotion could be achieved after nine consecutive months of good conduct – the reward being a more generous diet and extra exercise amongst other privileges. In 1923 the first step in the development of the 'classification of prisons' was introduced, with Wakefield becoming the first regional training prison. The main characteristics of the training prison were to develop good-quality prison industries, provision of vocational training in skilled trades and varied educational and recreational programmes. Wakefield also became the site of the Imperial Training School for prison officers in 1946 for the instruction of English, Scottish and Colonial prison staff.

Right: HM Prison New Hall Camp, built in 1936 in a clearing of woodland some miles outside of Wakefield, was the first open prison. The prisoners slept in wooden huts and the only boundaries were the whitewash marks on the trees. Only seven prisoners escaped between 1937 and 1952. The work undertaken by the prisoners was largely agricultural, although clearing woodland for cultivation and minor stock-raising of pigs, hens and rabbits was also carried out. This image shows inmates tending the gardens around their huts. In 1961 it was re-classified as a Senior Detention Centre which ran various regimes including the short, sharp shock system. It became a Local Prison and Youth Custody Centre for females in 1987, replacing the huts with two-storey accommodation blocks.

Below: The interior of one of the huts at HM Prison New Hall Camp. Inmates slept and ate in the huts, called 'messes', and were responsible for doing all their chores. This mess holds the Challenge Cup (as seen on the table) for the best kept mess.

Left: Air-raid damage to HM Prison Pentonville, after heavy bombing on the nights of 10 and 11 May 1941. At the outbreak of the Second World War as many prisoners as possible were discharged so as to be employed in war work, with some staff and senior boys from borstals joining the armed forces.

Below: An extract from the governor's Journal at HM Prison Pentonville for 10 May 1941. It outlines the extent of the damage to the prison from the bombing, and records that eleven prisoners, two prison staff and four prison staff family members were killed in the raid. Pentonville was one of five prisons considered to be situated in 'dangerous areas' during the war, and so were required to evacuate at the early stages of an emergency.

EXTRACT FROM GOVERNOR'S JOURNAL H.M.P. PENTONVILLE.

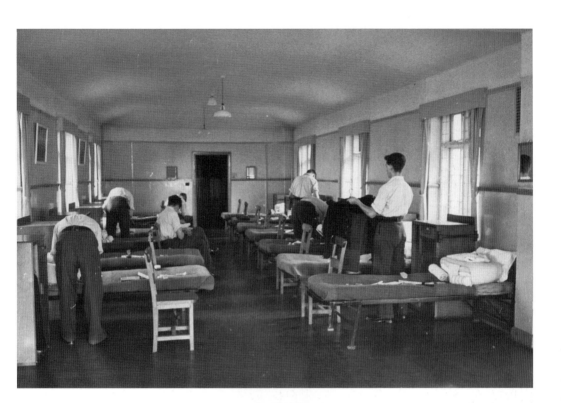

Above: One of the dormitories at
HM Detention Centre Goudhurst.
Prison policy in the post-war
years saw a shift from reform to
preventive sentencing with the
introduction of Detention Centres
and Remand Centres in 1948.
With an emphasis on discipline,
they are still used for the short-
term custody of young male
offenders aged between fourteen
and twenty-one.

Right: HM Remand Centre
Brockhill, Worchester, 1969.
Remand Centres were considered
not only as places of safe custody
for fourteen to twenty-one
year olds but also laboratories
for research into the causes and
treatment of juvenile delinquency.

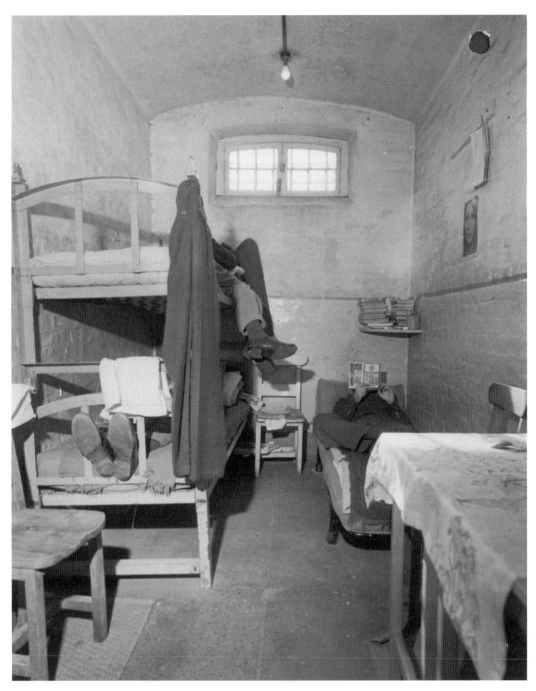

HM Prison Pentonville, 1969. Pentonville was the main inspiration for prison design in the nineteenth century, with its radial layout with four wings. It was built to accommodate the separate system which involved twenty-three hours of daily solitary confinement relieved only by an hour of exercise. In post-war Britain the prison population rose from 12,190 in 1945 to 20,474 by 1950. In order to accommodate this increase the concept of 'threeing up' was introduced, with three prisoners sharing a cell originally designed for the solitary confinement of one prisoner.

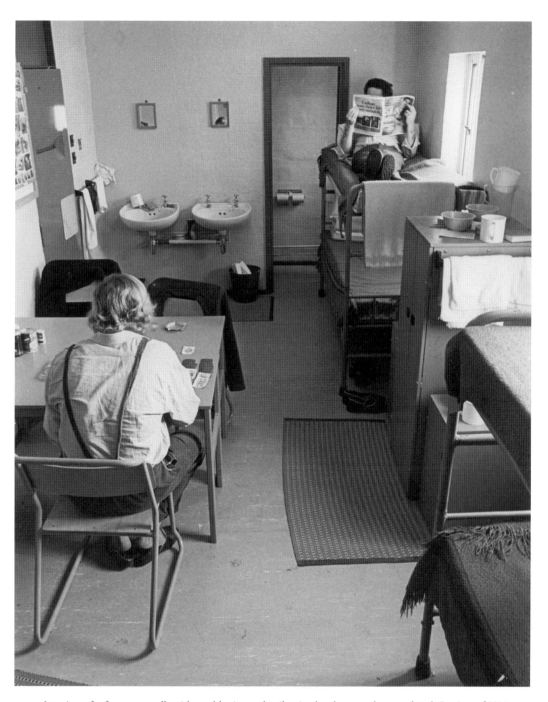

Interior of a four-man cell, with washbasins and toilet, in the then newly completed C wing of HM Prison Bristol, 1976. Refurbishment of prisons as a means of accommodating the ever-increasing numbers of inmates was one of many initiatives instigated during the 1970s to improve conditions for staff and inmates. Eighty-two establishments were selected to receive varying degrees of interior refurbishing from simple redecoration to improvements in wing sanitation.

Above: Gallery wing at HM Prison Wandsworth. Established in 1851 to cater for overcrowding at Brixton Prison, Wandsworth cost £136,308 to build and provided 708 cells suitable for the separate confinement of prisoners. In 1878 it became the principal execution prison for South London and as such an execution apparatus was installed. All execution equipment from the 1920s onwards (until the abolition of capital punishment in 1969) was held at Wandsworth and despatched to other prisons when needed.

Left: Gallery wing at HM Prison Standford Hill. On the site of an ex-Royal Air Force station, it was first used as a prison in 1950. Its current accommodation was built in 1986. The design of these two galleried wings is not too dissimilar even though they were built 135 years apart.

two

Women and
Children

Above: Female inmates gardening under the watchful eye of the wardresses at HM Prison Gloucester, *c.* 1900. A distinct uniform with numbered badges for each class of female prisoners was used as a means of monitoring and differentiating between individual prisoners. This assisted the application of rewards or punishments as well as a form of degradation. The uniform was plain and simple with no room for vanity; ear-rings, curled hair and any other forms of finery were prohibited. Hair was cut short and to remain so throughout the period of imprisonment.

HM Prison Askham Grange inmates tending to the chickens in the late 1940s. Originally built in 1886, Askham Grange was the house of a Leeds factory owner; it became a women's prison in 1947. Prisoners were trained in needlework and embroidery. In 1948 the prisoner workforce, of around sixty, made 3,590 shirts and 1,000 green money bags for the Royal Mint. It is a minimum security training prison for about seventy female prisoners. The majority of inmates are first-time offenders, but a carefully selected minority of women who have already been to prison have been gradually introduced.

Right: HM Prison Hill Hall, 1960. These inmates are presenting a sketch as part of a concert organised by inmates to raise funds in aid of the World Refugee Year. An appreciation of music and drama was fostered through choirs, bands, gramophone clubs and dramatic societies. Prisoners were encouraged to stage one or two performances a year.

Opposite below: prison officers and inmates in the grounds at the rear of the main building at HM Prison Askham Grange, 1971. By the 1970s female prisoners were allowed the extra privilege of being able to wear their own clothes. This was less of a consequence of a more liberal regime for women, but rather that women were seen as less of a security risk than male inmates.

Above: Female prisoners with their babies in HM Prison Wormwood Scrubs taking their morning exercise during the 1890s. The children, like their mothers, wore a prison uniform, usually 'a spotted blue frock'. During this period any child born in prison was taken from its mother at nine months old and placed in a charitable institution till the end of the mother's sentence.

Left: HM Prison Holloway crèche, seen here during the 1940s, was converted from a former isolation ward in 1891-1892. Not all prisons during the nineteenth century had nurseries, but those that did had special dormitory accommodation for women and their children. Nowadays the mother and baby units in Holloway and Styal have places for eight to fifteen babies respectively, up to the age of one year. At Askham Grange children may live with their mothers until they are two or three years old. However, life in these units can be as regimented for the babies as for the women in the prisons.

Opposite: HM Prison Exeter: inmates' babies in their highchairs waiting for their dinner.

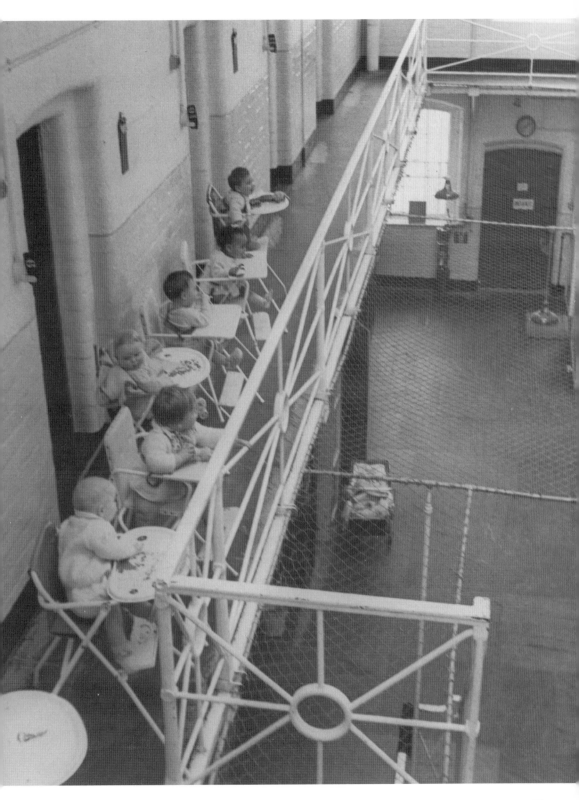

These two boys, one aged eleven and the other thirteen, where convicted in Portsmouth in 1899 for causing wilful damage to a door. They were sentenced to five days' hard labour. During the course of the nineteenth century there was a general movement towards greater protection of children and a trend to deal separately with the problem of juvenile delinquency. There had been an early move to separate young offenders within the prison system in 1838, with the use of the old military hospital at Parkhurst on the Isle of Wight. This was used to hold young offenders under the age of eighteen who had been sentenced to transportation. However, it was not until the state's recognition of Reformatory and Industrial Schools in the 1850s that the development of a separate legal process for children under the age of sixteen was put into effect. These schools provided an alternative to prison, offering moral, educational and vocational training as a means of steering them away from a life of crime. The next 100 years saw the amalgamation of Reformatory and Industrial Schools and the establishment of the Borstal and Detention Centres.

HISTORY AND PRISON RECORD OF JUVENILE-ADULT PRISONER.

(16 to 21 years of age.)

Register Number and Name ... 11394 William Jones

Age ... ... 16yrs Religion R.C.

Date and place of Birth ... ... 1890 Liverpool

Married or Single ... ... Single

Offence ... ... ① Stg 12 prs boots ② Stg a Jacket & vest

Date and place of Committal ... 6 Dec 06 Liverpool & Sssns

Date and place of Conviction ... do do

Sentence ... ... 3 & 3 Months H.L. (Consecutive)

Address of next of kin ... ... Parents 4/5 Cuvric St Lpool

Class of Labour for which fit ... Industrial labour

Previous Convictions and Sentences, including detention at Borstal or in any Reformatory, or Industrial School, with aliases ... .
> J.C. a 3-9-06 Not a/c Cups Saucers Everton Indusl School till 16yrs of age Stg mouth organ

School History, if any, and Standard, on conviction ...
> Attained to Standard V at Industrial School, character was indifferent - released 14/8/04 on licence

Character of Home ...
Are Parents living ? ...
> Parents intemperate - several times convicted of Drunkenness to - both charged with rec'g propy stolen by their son - Mother sentenced to 1 Mo - father disch'd mother sold up home - father in lodgings 4 children kept by grandmother

Knowledge of Trade, if any, and previous life ... ...
> Was taught Shoemak'g at the Indus School Casually employed rivet heating

Name and address of former employer ... ...
> Employed rivet-heating by C. Howson & Co 163 Regent Rd Lpool

No. 730 (9445)

Conviction history and prison record of William Jones, aged sixteen, sentenced to three months imprisonment and three months hard labour for stealing twelve pairs of boots, a jacket and a vest.

Above: Boys in the schoolroom at Werrington Junior Approved School for Boys in 1945, where education was considered the principal means of reform. Werrington was originally an Industrial School established in 1868. However, in 1933 Industrial and Reformatory Schools were renamed Approved Schools. They were intended for the education and training of boys and girls between the ages of ten and seventeen, sent to them by the courts either as young offenders or as needing care and protection. The boys at Werrington received an elementary education with a strong practical bias – pottery was the main craft taught. Pre-vocational work in farming, gardening, domestic and maintenance work was also provided. In 1955 the Prison Commission purchased the school and opened it as a Senior Detention Centre in 1957. In 1985 it was converted to a Youth Custody Centre and by 1988 it had become a Juvenile Centre for fifteen to seventeen year olds.

Opposite above: The schoolroom at HM Borstal Institution Rochester, 1907, the first borstal. Following one of the recommendations of the Gladstone inquiry in 1895, Sir Evelyn Ruggles-Brise, Chairman of the Prison Commission, introduced an experiment with young offenders from various prisons in London aged sixteen to twenty-one. The system was first tried out at Bedford Prison, but in 1902 the old convict prison at Rochester, near the village of Borstal, became the first closed (secure) borstal which accepted young offenders aged between fifteen and twenty-one years of age. The mental, physical and vocational training provided was for the purpose of reforming inmates, or 'lads' as they were often referred to, and preparing them for employment upon release. Above the gateway of Rochester Borstal can be found the following inscription in honour of its founder: 'He determined to save the young and careless from a wasted life of crime. Through his vision and persistence, a system of repression has been gradually replaced by one of leadership and training. We shall remember him as one who believed in his fellow-men.'

Opposite below: The boys' allotment and marble alley at Werrington Junior Approved School, 1945.

Left: North house dining hall at HM Prison and Borstal Institution Feltham. Feltham had originally been a local authority Industrial School but due to a rise in the number of committals a second borstal was required, therefore it was redeveloped and opened as a borstal in 1911.

Below: This famous march in 1930 of lads from Feltham Borstal to Lowdham Grange in Nottinghamshire epitomised the borstal movement. The lads camped on a hillside and were employed in the building of the first open borstal at Lowdham Grange. This was the fourth borstal to be opened and their slogans in the 1930s were 'Aim High' and 'Stickability'.

Borstal lads setting off on a trek as part of the Duke of Edinburgh Award Scheme, HM Borstal Institution Hewell Grange, Worcestershire, March 1969. The Duke of Edinburgh Award Scheme was introduced into borstals during the late 1960s, although camps had been a part of the borstal training system prior to this. Housemasters were in charge of the camps, and sought to ensure that every minute of the day was gainfully filled, usually with work, games and expeditions.

HM Borstal Institution Hewell Grange lads setting up camp, March 1969.

Left: A borstal girl assisting an outside building contractor at HM Borstal Institution East Sutton Park, 1962. This was the first purpose-built female borstal in England, opened in 1946. It is housed in a Grade II-listed country mansion and is now used to hold both adult and young female offenders in open conditions. It provides dormitory conditions of twenty-one rooms each catering for between two and thirteen girls. Training courses in gardening and farming, physical education and various community-based programmes are provided.

Below: HM Borstal Institution East Sutton Park laundry work in the 1940s.

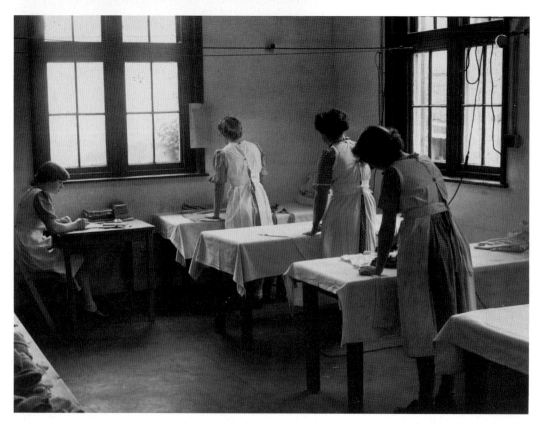

three

Daily Life

To aid identification, various physical characteristics of the convict were recorded, ranging from eye colour to the size of the person's head. Measurements for female prisoners were recorded by female warders. Here a prisoner is having his height measured at HM Prison Pentonville in 1865. On the desk is a calliper to measure the diameter of the head.

Right: The prisoner's details and description were entered into a register similar to this one from HM Prison Brixton, 1869-1872.

Opposite above: The vehicle traditionally used to transport prisoners was known as the Black Maria. The name is said to have originated from a lady named Maria Lee, who was a lodging-house keeper in Boston, Massachusetts in the 1830s – she reportedly used to escort inebriated people to the cells for the local constables. This Black Maria, shown outside Wormwood Scrubs, dates from 1895, although the first such prison van was commissioned in 1858.

Opposite below: Although the outside appearance of the Black Maria altered over the years, its capacity to transport prisoners changed little – each model contained twelve individual cells measuring 24 inches square. In the 1970s white vans began to replace the Black Maria, and in 1995 the Prison Courts Escorts Service was contracted out. The Black Maria pictured here dates from 1964.

No. 555.

Brixton PRISON.

4 February 1869.

SIR,

I beg to inform you that Register No. 1120 Sarah Geal will be discharged on the 5 of February 1869 from this Prison to the 20 Cambridge Road Mile End.

Please to sign the accompanying Certificate if he reports himself, and

DESCRIPTION.

Regr. Number, Name and Age) 1120 Sarah Geals (45)

Date and Place of Committal) 25 July 1865 Worship Street

Date and Place of Conviction) 18 Sept 1865 C.C.C.

Crime .... Attempting to discharge a loaded Pistol with intent &c

Sentence ...... 5 Years P.S.

Complexion .... Fair

Hair .... Dark Brown

Eyes .... Dark Hazel

Height........ 4 ft. 11 in

Marks .. .. Slightly Pockmarked

Date of Discharge 5th February 1869

Destination See above

Your obedient Servant,

Governor.

To The Governor
Horsemonger Lane Gaol
Southwark

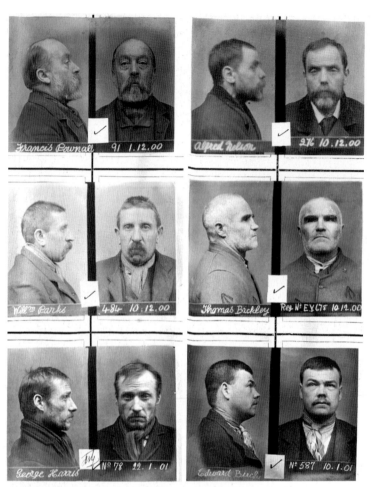

Francis Pownall 91 1.12.00

Alfred Nelson 276 10.12.00

Will™ Parks 484 10.12.00

Thomas Bickley Reg N° EYC78 10.12.00

George Harris N° 78 22.1.01

Edward Birch N° 587 10.1.01

Once the use of photography had become widespread it was possible to take 'mugshots' of the convicts. Some would try to avoid identification by scrunching up their faces or by putting pebbles in their mouths. Prisoner's hands were held up so any disfigurements could be noted. At the same time mugshots were being introduced in the prisons, some people were calling for newer, harsher measures to be employed to identify criminals, including the re-introduction of branding. Mugshot album 1898-1903 (unknown prison).

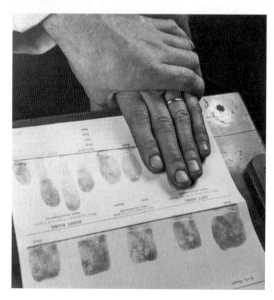

Left: It was only when fingerprinting was introduced that there was any accuracy in identifying convicts. However, this was not without its faults, as assistance from the prisoner was required to ensure that prints did not end up as little more than smudged black marks. Here the correct method of fingerprinting is being demonstrated at HM Prison Wandsworth in 1945.

Opposite: HM Prison and Borstal Institution Feltham. Prisoners' supplies are kept in the central stores, and issued upon arrival by a prison officer. There are also the part-worn stores, which hold a surplus of all equipment and can be used as a reserve in times of an unusually high prison population.

THE DISTINCTIVE DRESS OF VARIOUS CLASSES OF CONVICTS.

All the clothing up to number 5 is yellow. Reading from left to right the clothing indicates :—(1) First stage (first twelve months); (2) second stage (two years), black stripes on cuffs; (3) third stage (three years), yellow stripes on cuffs; (4) fourth stage, intermediate man, blue stripes on cuffs, chevron on cap and arms; (5) star man, blue stripes on cuffs, star on each arm and on cap; (6) grey dress worn by long-sentence men who earn 2s. 6d. a month and spend 1s. 3d. on comforts; (7) blue dress for good character; (8) black parti-coloured dress worn as punishment for striking an officer; (9) yellow parti-coloured dress, the penalty for running away; (10) canvas dress for those who destroy the ordinary clothing of their class.

[Reproduced by permission of the Proprietors of "Lloyd's News."]

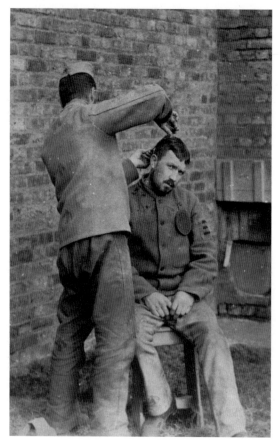

Above: The Victorians found it important to degrade prisoners, and clothing was just one way of doing this. Different uniforms were issued to distinguish between types of prisoners, as this illustration shows, though all the designs contain the broad arrow (to symbolise that the clothing belonged to the government, and was easily recognisable should the convict escape). The fact that the clothing often did not fit cannot have helped the prisoner's self-esteem either. The broad arrow was abolished from prisoner uniform in 1922, and now only convicted male prisoners are required to wear regulation clothing.

Left: Hair used to be cropped short on arrival, as shown here at HM Prison Wormwood Scrubs, *c.* 1900. This was to avoid the spread of lice, but also served to take away the prisoner's individuality. This practice has now been abolished, although all prisoners are encouraged to have regular trims.

RULES

Read to each Prisoner

ON ENTERING THE PRISON.

Every Prisoner is required to keep his person and furniture perfectly clean ; and not to mark, destroy, or disfigure any of the Books, Cards, Clothing, Bedding, or anything belonging to the Prison. He is to keep his Cell particularly clean, and to dust the cards and walls every day with his hand-brush ; to wash himself at least once a day, and to be ready to attend CHAPEL every morning when the Chapel-bell rings, except those who are of a different persuasion to the CHURCH OF ENGLAND, who are exempt, and by making proper application their own Minister will be allowed to attend them. No prisoner shall turn his head round to look behind him either in Chapel, Airing Ground, Corridor, School, or in any other part of the Prison. They are neither to sing, whistle, talk, sign to any other prisoner, or make a noise of any kind either in or out of the Cells. The Officer in charge of the wing will explain to each prisoner the amount and description of work he will have to do The Surgeon sees each prisoner once a week, viz., on Wednesday, and asks if they are well, and their reply must be either "YES" or "No," as the case may be. Prisoners to inform the Officer, when he opens the door first thing in the morning, if he wishes to see the Surgeon (who attends for that purpose), the Governor, or Chaplain. If a prisoner be purged, either night or day, he must ring his bell and medicine will be given to him by the Officer on duty. Each prisoner to wash his feet every Saturday forenoon, and to be standing with his shoes and stockings off, in order to shew them when the Officer opens his door for the purpose of giving him his dinner; a bell will be rung previous to inspection. Prisoners are to rise at half-past five, a bell being rung to announce it, and not to go to bed till the bell rings at eight o'clock ; and to sleep in nothing but his shirt The Governor will be ready at any time to hear the complaints of prisoners, should they desire to see him. A Visiting Magistrate goes round the Prison the third Thursday in each Month. Spitting is strictly prohibited.

WILLIAM AINSLEY and BROTHER, Letter-press and Lithographic Printers, Wholesale Stationers, &c., North Road, Durham.

On arrival at prison, new inmates were 'read the rules'. These had to be remembered to avoid punishment, however as this was often a long, drawn-out process, the first rules could sometimes be forgotten by the time the last ones were read out. To avoid this, prisoners are now issued with a handbook that contains all the rules and regulations.

Whilst routine varies widely between various types of prison, each one has its own strict daily schedule. These aim to ensure prisoner discipline and thus make the prison easier to run. They are often set out on signs such as this from HM Detention Centre Eastwood Park, 1969.

A typical morning scene at HM Prison Brixton in 1973. With no toilets in the cells, chamber pots were provided for prisoners locked up overnight. HM Prison Leeds was the last prison to abolish 'slopping out', which it did on Friday 12 April 1996.

Opposite above: It is the responsibility of the prison officers to ensure that the strict daily routines are adhered to and order is kept throughout the prison. As prison officers work in shifts, communication between each team is essential so that ongoing issues can be resolved. Here two senior officers from HM Prison and Borstal Institution Feltham can be seen handing over their duties.

Opposite below: A lot of work goes on behind the scenes in a prison. As the prison population increases, so does the amount of administrative work to be done, dealing with communication with the police and courts, ordering and accounting for all food and supplies for the prison. Here we see the administration offices at HM Prison and Borstal Institution Feltham.

Left: Prison kitchens are staffed by specialised grades of prison officers. They plan menus and supervise the prisoners that prepare, cook and serve all the meals for the whole prison. This kitchen at HM Prison Feltham was built by the prisoners.

Below: Prisoners used to eat their food in their cells, but now, where possible, they eat in communal (association) surroundings, normally a canteen, often with a choice of menu. This is a dinning room from one of the wings at HM Prison Wakefield in the 1940s.

TABLE OF DIETARIES
FOR PRISONERS
In the Gaol and House of Correction
Of the Borough of Portsmouth,

As Certified by the Secretary of State on the 26th September, 1863.

Class 1.

Convicted prisoners confined for any term not exceeding seven days:—

	Males		Females	
Breakfast,	Oatmeal gruel ...	1 pint	Oatmeal Gruel	1 pint
Dinner	Bread	1 lb.	Bread	1 lb.
Supper	Oatmeal gruel ..	1 pint	Oatmeal Gruel ...	1 pint

Class 2.

Convicted prisoners for any term exceeding seven days, and not exceeding twenty-one days:—

	Males			Females	
Breakfast	{ oatmeal gruel	1 pint }	oatmeal gruel ...	1 pint
	{ bread	6 oz. }	bread	6 oz.
Dinner	bread	12 oz.	bread	6 oz.
Supper	{ oatmeal gruel ...	1 pint }	oatmeal gruel ...	1 pint
	{ bread ...	6 oz. }	bread	6 oz.

Prisoners of this class employed at hard labour to have in addition, 1 pint soup per week.

Class 3.

Convicted prisoners employed at hard labour for terms exceeding twenty-one days, but not more than six weeks ; and convicted prisoners not employed at hard labour for terms exceeding twenty-one days, but not more than four months:—

	Males			Females	
Breakfast,	oatmeal gruel, 1 pint }		oatmeal gruel	1 pint
	bread ... ... 6 oz. }		bread ...	6 oz.
Sunday and {	Dinner.—soup ...	1 pint }	soup ...	1 pint
Thursday ... {	bread ...	6 oz. }	bread ...	6 oz.
Tuesday and	cooked meat without bone, 3oz. }		cooked meat, without	
Saturday ...	bread ... ... 6 oz. }		bone	3 oz.
	potatoes ... ... ½ lb. }		bread...6 oz. potatoes ½ lb.	
Monday,	{ bread ... ... 6 oz. }		bread	6 oz.
Wednesday,	{ potatoes ... ... 1 lb. }		potatoes ...	1 lb.
and Friday				
	Supper.—same as breakfast.		same as breakfast.	

Class 4.

Convicted prisoners employed at hard labour for terms exceeding six weeks, but not more than four months ; and convicted prisoners not employed at hard labour for terms exceeding four months:—

	Males			Females	
Breakfast—	oatmeal gruel 1 pint }		oatmeal gruel ...	1 pint
	bread ... 6 oz. }		bread	6 oz.
Sunday,	Dinner—cooked meat,		Cooked meat, without bone	3 oz.
Tuesday,	{ without bone 4 oz. }		potatoes	½ lb.
Thursday, &	{ potatoes ... ½ lb. }		bread	6 oz.
Saturday.	{ bread ... ... 6 oz. }			
Monday,	{ Soup ... ... 1 pint }		Soup	1 pint
Wednesday,	{ bread ... 6 oz. }		bread	6 oz.
and Friday				
	Supper.—same as breakfast.		same as breakfast	

Class 5.

Convicted prisoners employed at hard labour for terms exceeding four months :—

	Males			Females	
Breakfast—	Oatmeal gruel 1 pint {		Oatmeal gruel ...	1 pint
	Bread ... 6 oz. {		bread	6 oz.
Sunday,	{ Dinner—cooked meat, }		cooked meat, without bone	3 oz.
Tuesday,	{ without bone 4 oz. }		potatoes	½ lb.
Thursday and	{ potatoes ... 1 lb. }		bread	6 oz.
Saturday.	{ bread ... ... 6 oz. }			
Monday	{ Breakfast—oatmeal gruel 1 pint }		Oatmeal gruel ...	1 pint
Wednesday	{ Bread ... ... 6 oz. }		Bread ...	6 oz.
and	{ Dinner.—soup ... 1 pint }		soup	1 pint
Friday	{ potatoes ... ... 1 lb. }		potatoes ...	½ lb.
	{ bread ... ... 6 oz. }		bread	6 oz.
	Supper— Oatmeal gruel... 1 pint		Oatmeal gruel ...	1 pint
	Bread ... 6 oz.		Bread ...	6 oz.

Class 6.

Prisoners sentenced by Court to solitary confinement.

Males	Females
The ordinary diet of their respective classes	The ordinary diet of their respective classes.

Class 7.

Prisoners for examination, before trial, and misdemeanants of the first division, who do not maintain themselves :—

Males	Females
The same as class 4.	The same as class 4.

Class 8.

DESTITUTE DEBTORS.

Males	Females
The same as class 4.	The same as class 4

Class 9.

Prisoners under punishment for prison offences for terms not exceeding three days : 1lb. of bread per diem.

Prisoners in close confinement for prison offences under the provision of the 42nd section of the Gaol Act :—

	Males	Females
Breakfast...	Gruel—1 pint ; bread—6 oz.	Gruel—1 pint ; Bread—6 oz.
Dinner ...	Bread—6 oz	Bread—6 oz.
Supper ...	Gruel—1 pint ; bread—6 oz.	Gruel—1 pint ; Bread—6 oz.

NOTE.—*The soup to contain per pint, 3 ounces of cooked meat without bone, 3 ounces of potatoes, 1 ounce of barley, rice, or oatmeal, and 1 ounce of onions or leeks, with pepper and salt. The gruel to contain 2 ounces of oatmeal per pint. The gruel on alternate days to be sweetened with ¾ oz of molasses or sugar, and seasoned with salt. In seasons when the potatoe crop has failed 4 oz. of split peas made into a pudding may be occasionally substituted, but the change must not be made more than twice in each week.—Boys under 14 years of age to be placed on the same diet as females.*

JOHN ASTRIDGE, Governor.

In the Victorian era, the food in prison was used to reinforce the idea that prison life should be hard. However, maintaining necessary levels of fitness to allow prisoners to cope with the hard labour imposed on them as part of their sentence was also required. This Table of Dietaries from 1863 for the Portsmouth area shows the typical prison diet for the time. In prisons today the diet is balanced and nutritious. Special diets can also be arranged based on medical or religious grounds.

The Prison Service has always acknowledged the need for prisoners to undertake physical exercise. These boys had forty minutes of physical training every morning at HM Prison and Borstal Institution Feltham. Forced exercise like this may well have been a welcome break from confinement inside all day.

Work has always played an important part in prisoners' daily routines, with its function evolving throughout history. Here is a works party from HM Prison Wormwood Scrubs in 1895.

A prison visit in progress in the visiting room at HM Prison Blundeston, 1969. It is important to allow prisoners to keep close ties with their family and friends so that reintegration back into society is made easier. Whenever practicalities allow, prisoners with longer sentences are allocated to a prison near to their home. This is not always possible though, and some visitors are required to travel substantial distances for visits.

Ideally visits are organised within the sight and hearing of a prison officer, however due to the cost and feasibility of this it is not always possible. Where this is the case, closed visiting boxes are used, as seen here at HM Remand Centre Risley, c. 1965.

Prisoners have a statutory right to send one letter a week. Sending more than one letter is not always possible as all convicted prisoners' letters must be censored by prison officers. There are however no limits to the amount of letters prisoners in open prisons can send as their mail is not censored. This image shows prisoners at HM Prison Sudbury posting their letters into a post box at the prison.

Inmates are encouraged to spend their spare time, whether in the evenings or at weekends, in personal and intellectual development. This has been encouraged since the Second World War, and is now an integral part of the rehabilitation of prisoners. This scene shows the reading room at HM Prison Hill Hall around 1955, which was an open prison for women.

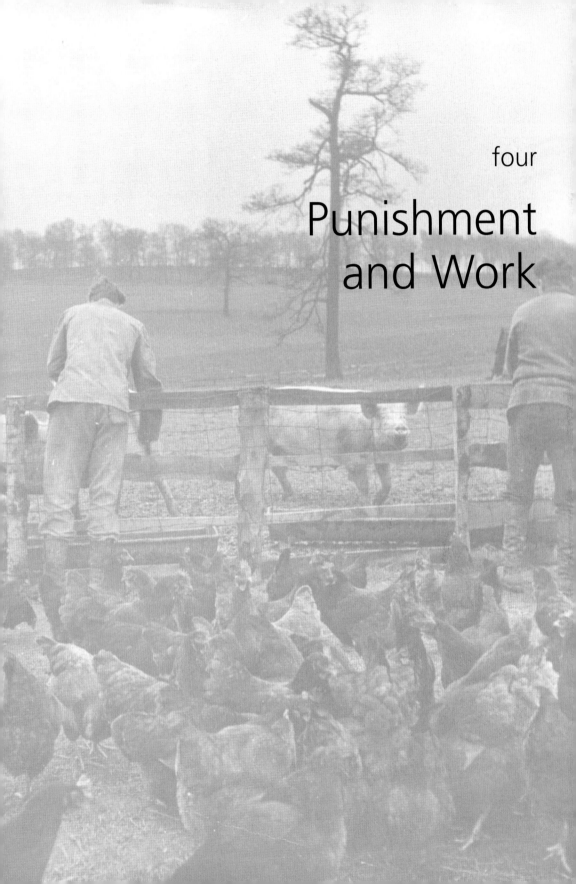

four
Punishment
and Work

At first work in prisons was purely punitive and supposed to act as a deterrent. It was divided into unproductive and useless labour. This photograph shows an inmate from Wormwood Scrubs turning the crank. The crank was a machine with a handle that had to be turned a certain amount of times a day (which was 10,000 at HM Prison Coldbath Fields) and was a form of useless labour. If the inmate seemed to be turning the handle too easily a prison officer would tighten a screw to make the handle harder to turn; hence the nickname of 'screw' for prison officers.

Another form of useless labour was picking oakum, which was more suitable for those who were unfit for the heavier work due to age, gender or disability. This involved sitting and picking old tar-soaked rope apart for hours on end like this prisoner at HM Prison Wormwood Scrubs, c. 1890. The unpicked rope was then used for calking ships, and so actually had a purpose. The intention of useless labour was to break both the body and spirit of the prisoner.

Opposite: The treadmill was invented by Mr Cubitt and was first used in HM Prison Brixton in 1817 as a form of useless labour. This handbill, printed in the 1820s, outlines the positive aspects of the treadmill and how it proved to be so beneficial at Brixton that other prisons had treadmills installed soon thereafter.

THE TREAD-MILL.

A Description of
The Tread-Mill.
" O word of fear,....Unpleasing to a Gamester's ear !"

THE Tread-Mill at Brixton, that " terror to evil-doers,"
has excited so much attention, that a correct view and
description of it, cannot fail of being acceptable to the public.
The Tread-Mill is the invention of Mr Cubitt*, of Ipswich,
and is considered a great improvement in Prison discipline ; so
much so, that since its beneficial effects have been experienced
at Brixton, mills of a similar construction have been erected at
Cold-Bath-fields, and several places in the country.

The above engraving exhibits a party of prisoners in the act
of working the Brixton Tread-Mill, of which it is a correct
representation.   The view is taken from a corner of one of the
ten airing yards of the prison, all of which radiate from the
Governor's house in the centre ; so that from the window of
his room he commands a complete view into all the yards.

To provide regular and suitable employment for prisoners
sentenced to hard labour, has been attended with considerable
difficulty in many parts of the kingdom : the invention of the
Discipline Mill has removed the difficulty, and it is confidently
hoped, that as its advantages and effects become better known,
the introduction of the Mill will be universal in Houses of
Correction.

* This gentleman's name has given rise to some jokes on the subject, among
such of the prisoners as can laugh at their own crimes, who say they are
punished by the cubit....Mon. Mag.

[Prison Scene.] Tom, Jerry, & Logic, ushered into their Country House.

Turnkey.....Come, gentlemen, off with your Dandy togs ; here's good rig-
ging of county grey, yellow flockings and clogs, for you ! In ., gentlemen,
here's loafers a-piece ; you'll each get another to-morrow morning, and there's
the pump, gentlemen, you are welcome to refresh yourselves as often as you
please ! Now, gentlemen, you must take a little exercise upon the wheel !

Tom.....Well, boys, we've napt it at last ; we've had some rare larks lately
among watchmen, prigs, blowings, codgers, &c., now we are captur'd with
the Greeks, and must be millers for this month to come ! Come, Jerry, my
boy, don't be down on your luck ; we must take the four with the sweet !

Jerry....I would not care a pin about the confinement, if it were not for
the confounded Mill, and short allowance ; what with these heavy clogs, and
constant treading, I fear that before my mouth is up I shan't have a bit of skin
upon my poor feet. If I were hale out again, I'll take care the gaming-table
shall not see my face in a hurry ! What say you, Logic ?

Logic....Why, my kids since we can't better ourselves we must be content
with our luck---it is needless to complain ; We have had a pretty good spell
lately ; I always thought the pigs would nick us, and so they have. However we must take better care for the future how we mix with the black legs ;
and, in the midst of our sprees always have
The fear of the Tread-Mill before our eyes.

Printed and Sold by J. CATNACH, 2, Mon-
mouth-Court, 7 Dials....[Price One Penny.]

A NEW SONG
Tom, Jerry, and Logic in the Tread-Mill.

THE Marriage Act, in daggerel verse, we've sung 'till all is blue,
    New we must try to entertain the town with something new ;
Is Jerry, Tom, and Logic, landed at the Treading-Mill.
        With their dash along, flash along, let them lark who will,
        But boys beware, look sharp, take care, or you'll nap the Treading-Mill.
There ne'er was known in London three such renowned sparks,
For fighting with the pales, and flooring charlies in the dark ;
At smashing lamps and knockers how surprising was their skill,
Now to complete their rakish feats, they're sent to Tread the Mill.
                With their dash along, &c.
One night a little boozy to a gambling-house they came,
Where the Greeks did soon persuade them to try a civil game ;
But the officers surpris'd them in the midst of mirth and glee,
And walk'd them to the watch-house where they had their quarters free.
Next morning they were taken before the Magistrate,
Who looking o'er the Vagrant Act did quick decide their fate,
He shook his head, and said, young men, the law for to fulfill,
I must commit you for a month to learn to Tread the Mill.
Of course poor Tom and Jerry at this look'd rather blue,
And must we go to Jail and mix among the ragged crew,
It pinches us most sadly to chew this bitter pill,
O curse on this hard fate of ours that we should Tread the Mill.
Then in a coach they cramm'd them and off to Quod they flew,
When the door was lock'd upon them their hearts nigh broke in two ;
Then each receiv'd a little loaf, allow'd them by the King,
With plenty water at command---but not a drop of---gin.
O then they were compelled to exchange their Dandy togs,
For grey jackets, yellow flockings, and a pair of thumping clogs,
When they began to Tread the Mill, Oh ! how their legs did ache,
You'd laugh'd t' have seen poor Logic, such wry faces he did make.
Now, in Limbo we must leave them, until their month is out,
To enjoy their bread and water and turn the wheel about ;
When at liberty again, should they be gaming be inclin'd,
" The terrors of the Treading-Mill" we trust they'll bear in mind.

Just Printed, a choice Assortment of Carols, with beautiful New Cuts.

Also, Life in London ; 44th Edition. New Marriage
Act, 30th Ed. The Last Day, 12th Ed.

As can be seen from this photograph, taken at HM Prison Wormwood Scrubs, the treadmill consists of steps set onto a cylinder which the prisoners then walk around. On average prisoners would do fifteen periods of fifteen minutes work each day. This meant that each prisoner would climb approximately 7,200 feet each day. Common health complaints from working on the treadmill included severe weight loss, varicose veins and aggravation of rheumatic and heart complaints.

Left: Although the treadmill originally had no purpose, many were adapted to have simple functions. These included ventilating the prison through operating windmills and drawing water. The book in the photograph, from HM Prison Gloucester, is a daily record of how much grain is milled by the prisoners. It is for the week commencing 3 August 1845.

After useless labour was abolished in the Prison Rules of 1899, it was decreed that all prisoner labour should be productive. It was also thought that the labour should try to make prisons more self-sufficient and therefore reduce costs to the Prison Service. Using prisoners to maintain Prison Service property is an ideal way to do this. Here a prisoner is refurbishing a window at HM Prison Lewes, 1971.

There is nothing new about the use of prisoners to maintain the buildings they live in, and it has even been extended to new wings, or even whole prisons, being built by prisoners. In this series of photographs you can see HM Borstal Institution Rochester being built entirely by inmate labour in 1902. This is still a common practice and is believed to be beneficial to the inmates. It is an ideal opportunity for them to gain on-the-job training as the work is carried out in conditions equivalent to a similar-sized commercial construction project.

Opposite above: Here you can see the bricks being made by hand, as was the custom at this time. Work on projects like this was done under the supervision of specialist prison officers known as trade officers. These officers normally have previous experience of working in the construction industry.

Opposite below: Here is the finished result. It is not only valuable for the inmates to do work like this, but it is also extremely beneficial for the Prison Service. When HM Detention Centre Eastwood Park was built, using the inmates from HM Prison Leyhill and HM Prison Bristol, it is estimated that the overall cost was 25 percent cheaper than it would have been if an outside contractor had been hired to do the job.

For many inmates, being in employment is an extremely important factor of being able to cope with a prison sentence. Often in life what we do makes us who we are and having something to pass the time and keep boredom away is crucial. Even mundane tasks, such as keeping the prison clean and tidy, give a sense of significance and can be used to teach the basic skills needed to lead a responsible law-abiding life. Here two prisoners are sweeping up at HM Prison Gloucester, *c.* 1900.

Opposite above: This is the laundry at HM Prison Wandsworth, *c.* 1950. Many prisoners whose sentences are too short, or cannot be trained in other areas, are set to work in the domestic services area of the prison, which includes employment in the laundry, kitchen and general cleaning. The washing for the whole prison is done in here, and often hospitals and other institutions send their laundry to the local prison to be cleaned.

Opposite below: Any catering training that inmates can receive in prison is valuable as it incorporates easily transferable skills useful for life after release. Here is a bread-making session at HM Prison Wakefield. This bread would be used in the prison diet. Although many prisoners are still employed in the kitchens, the majority of kitchens are now equipped with electric mixers and peelers to aid them in their work.

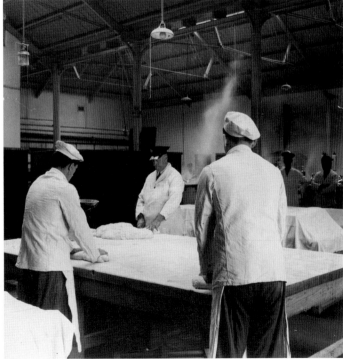

Above: Agriculture has been an integral part of convict labour, which was especially the case for HM Prison Dartmoor and HM Borstal Institution Rochester. These inmates at Rochester Borstal are off to milk the cows, *c.* 1910. After the Second World War there was a call to increase food production generally around the country, which the Prison Service rose to with an aim to become self-sufficient.

Left: The Prison Service has been able to reclaim derelict land which other farmers would often not have had the time or resources to work. This is due to the cheap labour costs that the Prison Service incurs. The land on which this inmate is feeding pigs at HM Prison New Hall Camp, 1947, was derelict until the camp was built in 1936.

Right: The value of the training inmates receive whilst doing agricultural work is under debate. Here at HM Prison and Borstal Institution Feltham the inmates are being trained in market gardening. However many of the people in prison are from urban areas and will be returning to urban areas when they are released, so it is questionable whether they will be able to put this training to any use. However it is arguable that the work ethos instilled in the inmates through any employment is valuable enough in itself.

Below: Although the value of the training is under debate, there is no question about the value of the produce that is the result of the farms. The majority of goods are used in the prison dietary, with any extra produce being sold on the open markets. Here, female inmates at HM Prison Holloway are making jam, *c.* 1966.

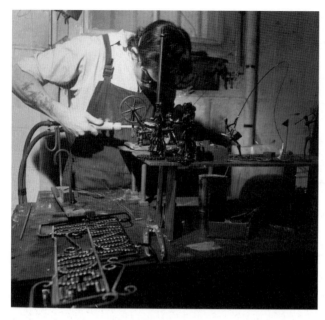

Left: With many prisons located in city centres it is not always possible to find the land to allocate to farming; consequently other employment must be found for the inmates. This is mainly done in the form of workshops, with both skilled and unskilled employment available. At HM Prison Dartmoor in 1972, an inmate works in the blacksmiths shop making souvenirs from pieces of scrap metal, which are to be sold locally.

Below: To enable the inmates to learn the new skills required to work in the workshops they attend evening classes. This inmate learnt his trade whilst incarcerated, and subsequently repaired the other inmates' shoes at HM Prison Dartmoor, 1972, in the Boot and Shoe Repair shop.

Right: Other skills can be taught during the workshop. At HM Detention Centre Latchmere House in 1966, an assembly shop is in progress with a prison officer instructing.

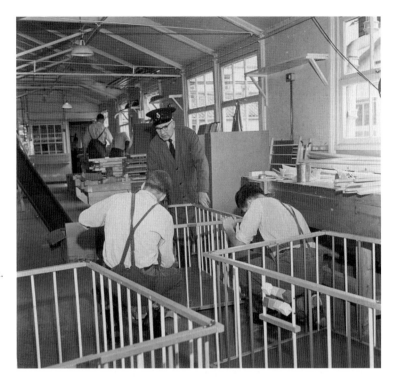

Below: The main problem with prison workshops is the need to keep pace with the rapidly developing world of industry that exists outside of prison. Making baskets like this is not as common a sight in prisons as it once was. HM Prison Dartmoor, *c.* 1900.

Making mail bags is one of the more stereotypical tasks that prisoners do. All prison industries are now incorporated under the commercial heading of Prindus, which was established in 1972.

Above: Prindus (Prison Industry) is a rapidly expanding area of the Prison Service, with more and more industries becoming a part of it every year, including assembly work, cloth making and engineering work. At HM Prison Coldingley, 1969, the inmates make road signs.

Right: The unskilled industry workshops are ideal for those who are only in prison for a short period, as they often require only simple, repetitive tasks. At HM Prison Wormwood Scrubs, 1963, the inmates make children's toys.

Left: An inmate clocks out after his day's work in the prison at HM Prison Gloucester, 1969.

Below: Some prisoners who are serving a term of four years or more are selected to work ordinary jobs in the community to ease them back into society and get them used to having their freedom. Here an inmate from HM Prison Pentonville swaps his prison identity card for a works pass, 1969. Not all prisoners are suitable for this scheme due to the nature of their offence or their behaviour whilst in prison.

Opposite above: When inmates do valuable work in the local community it can help to build the relationship between the prison and the surrounding neighbourhood, which can sometimes be a fragile one. A 'meals on wheels' service is run from HM Prison Kirkham, 1974, with over 1,000 meals a week being prepared by the inmates.

Opposite below: Working within the community with vulnerable people can also provide an opportunity for work experience that prisoners may not have considered under different circumstances. Three inmates from HM Prison Appleton Thorn, 1973, are working at Daresbury Hall Residential Centre, taking the residents for an outing in the grounds.

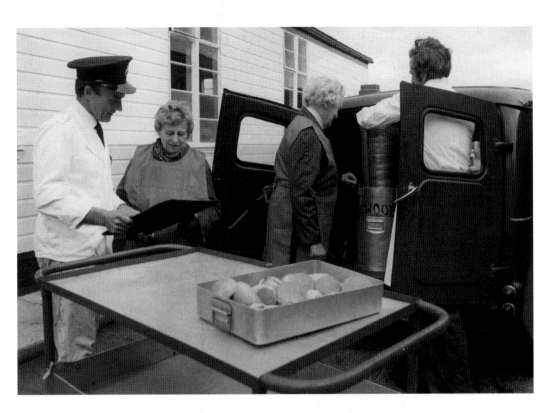

On the same principle that inmates are used to reduce costs within the Prison Service through maintaining and building its properties, the Government also uses inmate labour to reduce costs in its other departments. Here boys from HM Prison and Borstal Institution Feltham are packing stores for the Royal Army Ordnance Corps as part of the war effort, *c.* 1940.

Inmates make trawl nets at HM Prison Thorp Arch, 1975.

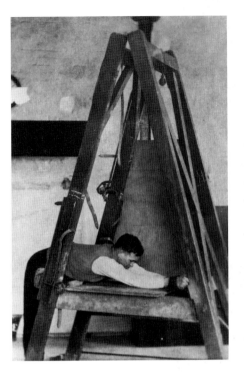

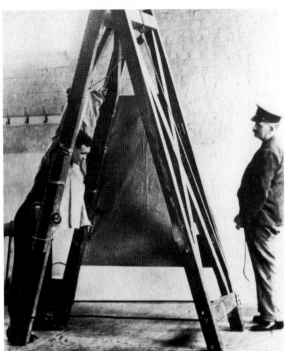

This series of photographs shows the whipping frame and the different ways of using it. Corporal punishment was used for serious breaches of the prison rules, for example assaulting a prison officer or inciting a riot. The flogging was administered with a 'cat-o'-nine-tails' or a birch. A cat-o'-nine-tails was a whip which normally had nine thongs fastened to a handle. A birch, on the other hand, was a bundle of sticks tied together. Corporal punishment was only abolished from English prisons in 1967. Now punishments generally consist of the removal of privileges or association time.

The system of punishment in modern-day prisons is much more complex than simply flogging someone. Forfeiture of remission is seen as the harshest punishment (the prisoner is made to serve their full sentence, thus surrendering the possibility of early release), followed by forfeiture of privileges, stopping earnings, and being excluded from associated work (where the inmate has to work in their cell). There is also cellular confinement. When a prisoner is on cellular confinement they are either kept in their own cell or on a special block known as a segregation unit and are only allowed out for exercise. This is the segregation unit at HM Prison Dartmoor, 1972.

This is a cell in the segregation unit at HM Prison Albany in 1984. In modern-day prisons all segregation cells must be furnished to the same basic level as normal cells. In reality the segregation unit is mainly used for prisoners on Rule 43. This rule is used to maintain good order and to protect vulnerable prisoners. Such prisoners are taken away from association, even though they have not done anything they need disciplining for. It can even be done at the prisoner's request.

five

Prison Staff

Above: Prison staff at HM Prison Gloucester, *c.* 1900. The governor, seen here at the front in civilian clothes, is responsible for the security and welfare of the prisoners and for the maintenance of prison discipline.

Left: Chief warder and warder, HMP Gloucester, *c.* 1900. The paramilitary staff structure had been used in the Convict Prisons since 1850. Local Prisons adopted it in 1877. The structure consisted of the following staff: governor; chief warder; principal warder; warder and assistant warder. The chief warder was the head of discipline and responsible for the division of duties among the staff and the location and employment of prisoners.

HER MAJESTY'S PRISON GLOUCESTER

PRINCIPAL WARDER GILES CAMBRIDGE

1858   Giles Cambridge-No.2 Treadmill Officer.

1860   Giles Cambridge-No.1 Treadmill Officer.

1861   Giles Cambridge-Head Officer of the Gaol.

1871   Giles Cambridge-Promoted to Principal Warder.

THE ABOVE PHOTOGRAPH WAS PROBABLY TAKEN IN 1871 ON GILES CAMBRIDGES PROMOTION. THE PHOTOGRAPHER WAS "SAMPSON S. SOLEY"-BRUNSWICK ROAD WHO TRADED IN GLOUCESTER BETWEEN 1865 – 1879.

Principal Warder Giles Cambridge, HMP Gloucester, *c.* 1871. Principal warders advised the governor on the day-to-day activities and happenings in the prison. They were responsible for maintaining discipline and coordinating their staff. A principal warder was assigned to each hall of a prison. In the larger prisons a principal warder would also be stationed at the centre of the prison to regulate the comings and goings of prisoners from the cells to the workshops.

Prison warder, HM Prison Gloucester, *c.* 1900. The minimum height for entry as a prison warder was 5 feet 8 inches and had to be between the ages of twenty-one and thirty-five. Warders in the early days worked up to fifteen hours a day and only received one Sunday off in every three. Their duties consisted primarily of locking and unlocking doors and gates, and the day-to-day supervision and monitoring of prisoners. In 1921 warders were renamed prison officers.

Right: Prison Warder John S. Maddock, HM Prison Leicester 1919-1925. He joined the Prison Service as a labourer at Wakefield Prison on 15 June 1896. He was promoted to assistant warder on 24 August 1897 and again to warder on 1 May 1904. He served at both HM Prison Leeds 1916-1919 and HM Prison Leicester 1919-1925. John Maddock was commended by the prison commissioners in December 1923 for his zeal and intelligence in effecting the re-capture of a prisoner who escaped from an escort, whilst he was serving at Leicester. He was awarded the Imperial Service Medal in 1925, presented to him by Colonel Knox, who later became Commissioner of the Prison Service.

Below: Two wardresses and the matron (pictured right), HM Prison Gloucester, *c.* 1900. Matron was the equivalent of a deputy governor and was responsible for the female section of the prison. The first mention of a matron in charge of female prisoners was that of Mrs Kent, who was dismissed from Gloucester Prison in 1800. The 1808 Prison Rules required prisons to appoint a salaried matron who was to be responsible for the prison linen and laundry, and the supervision of the female prisoners.

Prison staff at HM Prison Holloway, c. 1910. The great majority of prisons in the early nineteenth century had less than ten staff. In the 1830s and 1840s the staff primarily consisted of the governor, his wife (acting as matron), a few assistants or turnkeys, a visiting chaplain and a part-time surgeon. By the 1930s the staff at Holloway Prison included the governor, deputy governor, Anglican and Roman Catholic chaplains, male prison officers (whose work was confined to gate duty and managing the stores), female prison officers (who were responsible for the control and discipline of the prison) and medical and hospital staff which included female medical officers, hospital superintendents, sisters and qualified nurses.

Opposite above: Working party and warder at HM Prison Gloucester, c. 1900. The Works Department is responsible for the maintenance and repair of the prison and managing the stores. They are occasionally assisted by a small number of prisoners whom they are responsible for.

Opposite below: The Dominion and Colonial Prison Superintendents' Conference, HM Prison Wakefield, c. 1927. By the time of the First World War, Prison warders, selected by the Secretary of State for the Colonies, were seconded for service with the colonial prisons as far a field as Honduras, Jamaica, Cyprus and Nigeria. In 1927 the first Imperial Prison course for overseas prison officers was held at Wakefield Prison. In many instances the methods and principles seen in practice in this country were found suitable for adoption, modified to meet local circumstances, by prisons in different parts of the Empire.

Above: Practical instruction in court procedure, shown here at Leyhill in 1962, is just part of a prison officer's training. The full course includes lectures, prison visits, discussions, demonstrations and physical training. As early as 1856 the chaplain of Dartmoor Prison recommended the establishment of educational facilities for staff. Libraries and recreation rooms were set up to develop a corporate spirit amongst staff. The Gladstone Committee 1892-1895 recommended that two or more prisons should be set aside as training schools for all staff. The first school was established at HM Prison Chelmsford in 1896. The following year other schools were opened for warders at Hull and for wardresses at Wormwood Scrubs (afterwards transferred to Holloway Prison). Leyhill Officers' Training School was established in 1962 as a residential college for newly joined prison officers. After a month's practical training in a prison, trainee prison officers have to attend Leyhill for an eight-week course. The course is designed to teach students the basic skills they will require as prison officers, to provide them with a framework of knowledge of the Prison Service, and to give them some insight into the problems and needs of inmates.

Right: Prison officers attending a first-aid class, HM Prison Leyhill, 1980s.

Below: Probationers, 1908. Prison officers have to serve a twelve-month probation period before being confirmed in post.

Opposite below: Prison officers at HM Prison Leyhill being taught Judo, 1962.

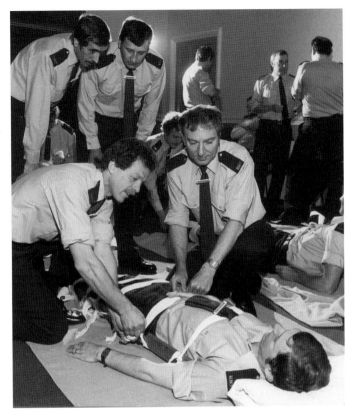

Probationers Feb. 1908

Above: Prison officers' club where officers and their wives and friends can relax in the evenings, HM Prison Leyhill, 1975. William Holderness, the chaplain at Dartmoor Prison in the early 1860s, argued that the absence of suitable educational facilities and areas for relaxation affected the quality of officers' work. It was not until 1878, at Portsmouth Prison, that the first reading and recreation rooms were officially provided.

Left: Time to relax and take a break in the staff dining room, HM Prison Leyhill, 1940s.

Opposite below: The Leyhill Prison Staff Military Band, 1952. Several prisons and borstals formed their own local amateur bands as means of recreation.

Above: Officers' quarters at HM Prison Holloway, 1962. Many local authorities insisted that subordinate officers and governors should reside in the prison or within a certain distance from the prison. The governor's house and chaplain's house were normally on either side of the entrance gates. The subordinate staff quarters tended to be close to the prison wall. Although some staff were fortunate to live in cottages or houses attached to the prison, most were in barrack-style buildings.

The famous pony patrol at HM Prison Dartmoor was introduced in 1902 to help tighten-up security. This image shows the final pony patrol which ceased operation in 1974.

As a result of a number of high-profile escapes from prisons in the 1960s, Lord Mountbatten undertook an enquiry to examine the reason for these escapes and to assess the level of security within prisons. The enquiry recommended a number of new security measures which included the introduction of dog patrols. This prison officer and his dog, 'Prince', at HM Prison Wormwood Scrubs in 1967, were one of the first dog handler teams to be deployed in the Prison Service. However, it is known that Gloucester Prison used dogs for some guard duties as early as 1820.

six

Security

Above: The first and foremost priority of the Prison Service is to hold its prisoners in secure captivity and therefore prevent escapes. Here you can see an escape attempt from HM Detention Centre Northallerton in early March 1946.

Below: This is the form that used to be filled out when someone escaped prison to aid their detection. Due to advances in technology these are no longer required. It was due to a spate of escapes that the Mountbatten inquiry was set up in 1966. The report that originated from this suggested a variety of security measures that needed to be changed.

DESCRIPTION OF

PRISONER JUST ESCAPED

From H.M. Prison,_____

Date and Hour of Escape	Name and Alias, Offence, Place of Conviction and Sentence	Born at	Age	Com- plexion	Hair	Eyes and Eyebrows	Build	Height Ft. Ins.	Trade	Dress Worn at Time of Escape	Distinctive Marks and Peculiarities, With Localities to which Prisoner may Proceed

Any persons who apprehend, and deliver up the Prisoner, may receive such reward as the Prison Department or Directors of Prisons may consider their services severally justify === not exceeding FIVE POUNDS in the whole.

Right: Signs, like this one at HM Prison Norwich, are posted outside the main entrance of all prisons. They outline some points from the Prison Act 1952, which covers the security of prisons. This includes how it is illegal to take anything in or out of prison, or to help prisoners escape.

Below: Not all prisons have the stereotypical closed main gate. The main gate at HM Borstal Institution Feltham looks more like that of a country manor than a prison. The security required at the main gate is normally determined by the type of prisoner contained within. Prisoners are categorised into one of four security categories, and are reassessed throughout the duration of their sentence. These categories were introduced by the Mountbatten Report.

The gatehouse is one of the most significant and visible parts of the prison, and so must be secure. As well as being a point of access to the outside world, they have also had a variety of functions throughout history. These range from containing reception facilities, the administration department or visiting rooms, through to having the governor's and chaplain's houses on either side. This picture shows the inside of the gatehouse at HM Prison Brixton, 1972.

The majority of prisons are divided into sections that have locked internal gates and doors separating them, like this one at HM Prison Wandsworth, 1972. This means that any disturbance can be contained within one section of the prison.

This photograph shows a works party from HM Prison Dartmoor quarrying at 'The Herne Hole', *c.* 1886. The guards with rifles were civil guards not prison warders. Civil guards were civilians, normally with previous military service, who undertook responsibility for the perimeter security of work parties and convict prisons. They were abolished in 1919.

The introduction of two-way radios aided security in prisons immensely, allowing continuous contact between prison officers in any part of the prison. Here the security principle officer uses his two-way radio at HM Prison Spring Hill, 1973.

With Officer Newton driving and Officer Sellick operating the radio, this prison van is preparing to enter the gate of HM Prison Leicester in 1976. With the risk of a breach of security increasing while transporting prisoners, constant communication between all parties is essential.

Right: Closed circuit television allows continual surveillance of the prison, and, because it is recorded, footage of any significant events can be used as evidence where needed. It also means surveillance can be increased using the minimal amount of staff. Even rudimentary technology, like the equipment shown here at HM Prison Blundeston in 1963, was highly effective.

However, even with extensive security systems, reliability still depends on the effective training and awareness of the staff using it.

This photograph, from 1973, shows students in a mock workroom being taught to look for hidden weapons and other contraband. The workshop areas in prisons provide one of the most vulnerable points in security, so extra care must be taken.

Drugs are a serious problem in prisons, and addressing this issue is a major challenge for the Prison Service. Here new officers are being trained in cell searching so that they can find concealed contraband. Cell searches are generally carried out every couple of weeks, depending on the prison.

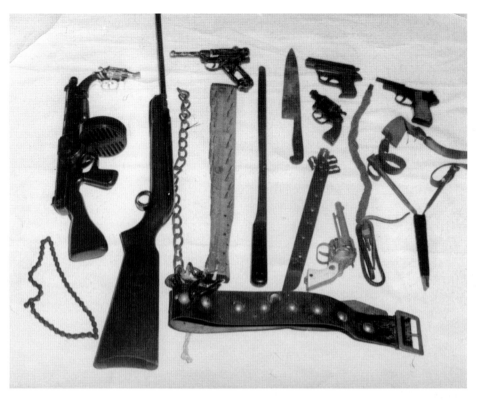

The range of prohibited items found in prisons can be quite astonishing, and an obvious security risk. These items found at HM Prison Wormwood Scrubs include several types of handguns, knives, a rifle and a plank of wood with nails stuck through it, though in general it is rare for items such as these to be found in prisons.

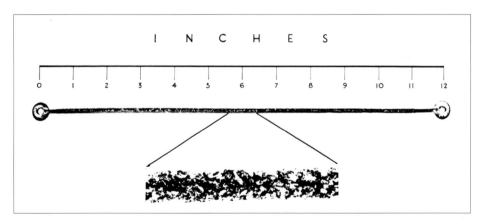

Occasionally something will come to light that demands extra security measures. In May 1968 an urgent memo was sent out highlighting the existence of a tungsten carbine rod. This is the picture that was included with that memo and it shows an example of the rod, with a section of it magnified seven times. It is able to cut through most alloys and all hard materials, and will fit a standard hacksaw. Obviously this proves an extremely high security risk and must be treated with appropriate measures.

This picture shows the aftermath of the Strangeways riot. In a response to the awful conditions in some local prisons, inmates at HM Prison Manchester, which at the time was called Strangeways, rioted and took control of the prison from 1 April 1990 to 25 April, which makes it the longest prison siege in history. During its course nearly 200 people were injured, both prisoners and staff. A prisoner and one prison officer later died in hospital as a result of their injuries.

The inquiry into the riot was conducted by Lord Justice Woolf, with the report being released in February 1991. It looked at six disturbances in other prisons and proposed a series of recommendations to try to avert such events from happening again.

seven

Body and
Soul

Hospital ward at HM Prison Holloway, 1940s. The female infirmary was constructed between 1891 and 1892. Additional hospital cells were added between C wing and the hospital in 1913. This included two padded cells, a ward for female officers, a surgery, a medical officer's room and kitchen, two wards, and a nurses' room. In 1919 the prison commissioners employed five fully trained nursing sisters in the hospital at Holloway.

Opposite: The hospital ward at HM Prison Holloway, 1940s. Medical care for prisoners was introduced through the Health of Prisoners Act 1774. This enabled local Justices, who were responsible for the running of prisons, to order the provision of sick-rooms and cleaning facilities, as well as to appoint a surgeon or apothecary. By the 1850s most London prisons had infirmaries. In 1902 the prison commissioners decided to establish a Prison Hospital staff. Candidates appointed to this element of the Prison Service were expected to pass through a probationary course of technical training in first aid and nursing. General surgeries were held daily and the women made appointments in a similar manner to outside. Today a full range of specialist services are provided including gynaecology, paediatrics, physiotherapy and dentistry.

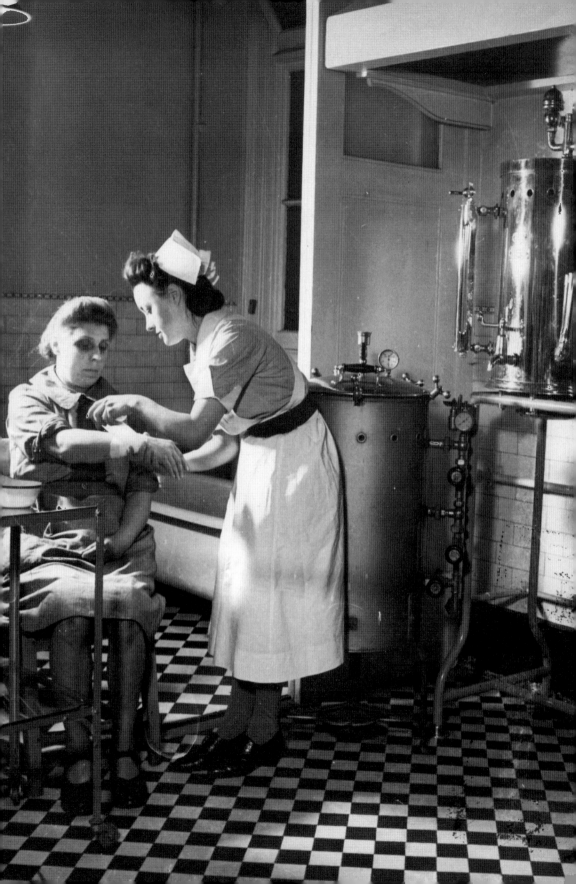

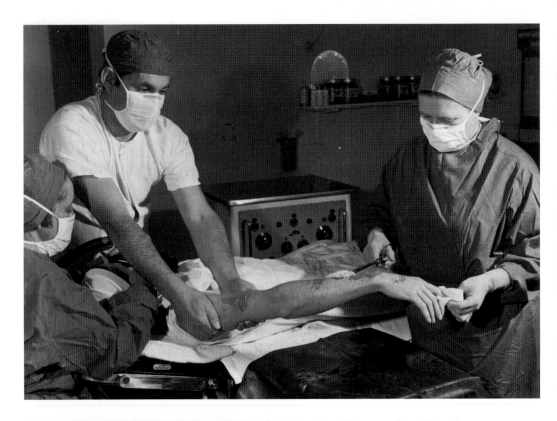

Above: Theatre staff sterilising the operation area prior to the surgical removal of an inmate's tattoos at HM Prison Grendon, 1970. A new technique for the removal of tattoos, derma-abrasion, was introduced by a medical officer in 1971 at HM Prison Liverpool.

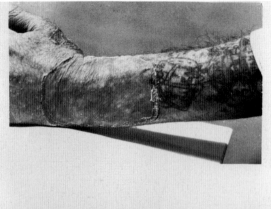

Left: Before and after images of a tattoo removal operation.

Opposite above: Those prisons that did not have the facility for dentist units would transport inmates to the local dental surgery for treatment. Here a party of young female offenders, from HM Borstal Institution East Sutton Park, is being taken to a local dentist, 1962.

Below: In the early twentieth century dental care was almost entirely neglected. One ex-prisoner, during this period, claimed that the only solution to a dental problem was the crude extraction of the tooth by an untrained warder. Although prisoners could obtain a toothbrush, this privilege was not well known among the prison population. Some prisons, such as Pentonville seen here, have dental units, which are staffed by civilian dentists who visit the prison once a month.

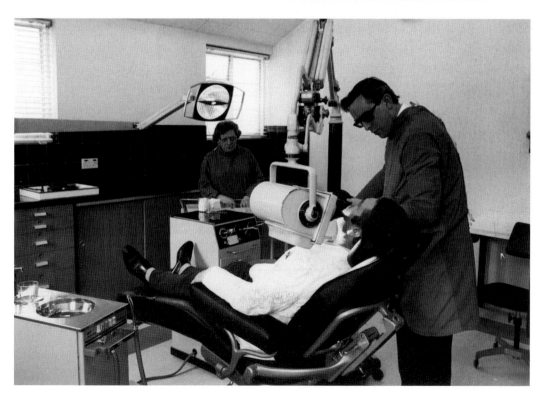

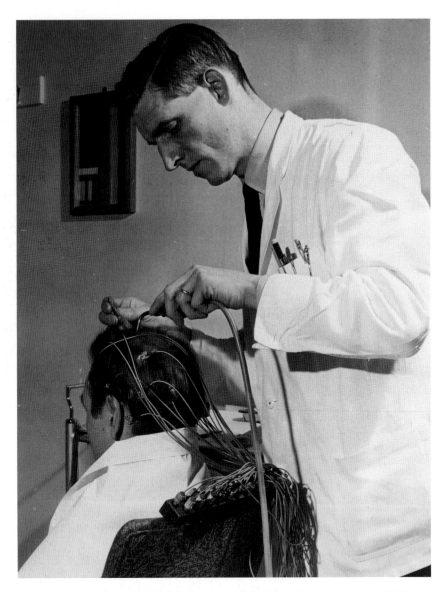

An electro-encephalography (EEG) technician applying electrodes to an inmate, HM Prison Grendon, 1970. Each new arrival receives an electro-encephalography examination, which records the electrical activity of the brain in order to identify any abnormalities. Provision for 'criminal lunatics' developed under separate legislation in the nineteenth century. The services were largely institutional and custodial. Criminal lunatics were received both into local lunatic asylums and into the special criminal lunatic asylum Broadmoor which opened in 1863. In 1946 the first psychiatric unit was opened at Wormwood Scrubs. HM Prison Grendon, however, was established in 1962 as an experimental psychiatric prison to provide treatment for prisoners with antisocial personality disorders. It has three objectives: to investigate and to treat offenders suffering from disorders; to investigate the mental condition of offenders the nature of whose offences suggest mental disorder; and to explore the problem of the psychopath in order to provide treatment or management to which he might respond.

Right: A visiting psychologist has an informal meeting with one of the boys at HM Borstal Institution Lewes, 1954. The psychologists in remand and trial prisons work with the prison's medical officers to assist them in the preparation of reports on the psychological condition of untried and convicted prisoners.

Below: A group counselling session with a prison officer at HM Prison Grendon, 1970. Group counselling was introduced in the late 1950s and 1960s in order to improve staff-inmate relationships, and involved a small group of inmates meeting with a member of staff once a week to discuss various topics.

Right and below: The chapel at HM Prison Wakefield, with its individual cubicles that adhered to the separate system used within the prison. On a Sunday there would be two Church of England services lasting around one hour each. Other than half an hour of exercise, chapel was the only respite from the monotony of solitary confinement. As a result attendance was high. This chapel was burned down during a fire at the prison in 1974.

Opposite above: Many of the boys on arrival to HM Borstal Institution Lowdham Grange are unfit and are therefore given remedial exercise. Trainees usually have approximately five hours of physical education a week. This includes training in certain recreational activities and instruction in sports such as football, rugby and gymnastics. Outward-bound activities such as camping are also organised, usually during the summer months.

Opposite below: HM Borstal Institution Feltham is set aside for those cases which, for some physical and mental reason, are considered in need of full-time care and attention from a highly trained medical staff. This image shows the hospital's solarium, a room fitted with extensive areas of glass designed for exposure to the sun and used for the treatment of illness by means of sun-baths.

The chapel at HM Prison Wormwood Scrubs, 1964. It is the largest Protestant chapel in a prison and stands directly opposite the main entrance acting as a screen from the prison's grim brick walls. Wormwood Scrubs was built by convict labour over sixteen years from 1874 to 1890. The stone for the chapel was quarried at Dartmoor and Portland convict prisons, the iron castings were made at Portland, and the carpentry, joinery and metalwork undertaken at Millbank and Chatham prisons. Around the central courtyard are cloisters of white Portland stone. The geraniums in the flowerbeds were a gift from Kew Gardens, where thirty prisoners were working. The chapel's interior was designed to accommodate the separate system, preventing the inmates from seeing each other during the service. The organ was built in the prison shops by prison labour – when it was discovered that there was a skilled organ builder among the inmates it was decided that an organ was to be made for the chapel.

An inside view of Wormwood Scrubs chapel. On the left of the picture is a piano that was presented to the prison by Ivor Novello, the Welsh-born actor, songwriter and dramatist. He served four weeks of an eight-week sentence at Wormwood Scrubs for the misuse of petrol coupons in 1944.

Chapel at HM Prison Gloucester, c. 1900. Above the alter, in the centre of the balcony, is a plaque with the initials IHS which is the symbolic monogram of the sacred name of Jesus and stands for 'Iesus Hominum Salvator' (Jesus Saviour of Men). In the late 1960s attendance at chapel ceased to be compulsory for prisoners.

The Roman Catholic chapel at HM Prison Holloway, around the 1950s. In some prisons, Roman Catholics and Anglicans were forced to use the same chapel, meaning that prisoners could only attend service on alternate days. Holloway, however, has both an Anglican and a Roman Catholic chapel. Amongst the various privileges that are bestowed on female prisoners, Roman Catholics are allowed a crucifix within their cell.

Right: Holy Communion at HM Prison Winchester chapel, 1981. Apart from ministering to the spiritual needs, as seen above and below, members of the Chaplaincy Department interview every prisoner on reception, visit sick and disturbed prisoners, and undertake the often distressing and difficult job of delivering bad news to individual prisoners.

Below: Father Pink hears confession from an inmate at HM Prison Holloway, 1981.

Opposite above: The synagogue at HM Prison Wormwood Scrubs. Jewish prisoners are exempt from labour on the Sabbath and their five principal festivals.

Opposite below: The religious needs of prisoners at HM Prison Holloway are catered for by the Chaplaincy Department, 1981. From left to right: a Sister from the Order of St Vincent de Paul, a full-time Church of England chaplain, a part-time Roman Catholic priest, and a Church of England deaconess. Ministers of other religions are encouraged to visit the prison to see members of their faiths including the Church Army, Methodists, the Rabbi, and many others. The Prison Act 1865 made provisions for the employment of Anglican chaplains. However the introduction of Roman Catholic priests was much slower, due to the continued anti-popery among the Anglican chaplains. Edmund Du Cane, Chief Prison Commissioner, increased the number of paid Catholic chaplains following the 1877 Prison Act. They are not appointed by the prison commissioners, but by the Bishop of the diocese.

The chaplain joins in the recreation period with inmates at HM Borstal Institution Wellingborough, 1964. Chaplains were also responsible for arranging various forms of entertainment for inmates as well as recommending books for the prison library.

Opposite: The chaplain has his own keys to the prison, and is able to visit an inmate in his cell at any time he is needed, as here at HM Prison Preston in 1973. However, due to the other duties and the number of inmates under his charge, the chaplain's visits are often short and infrequent, ranging from once a month to every six weeks.

The chaplain is one of the members of the Review Board, which assesses an inmate's suitability for transfer to an open establishment, parole, release or licence. HM Prison Preston, 1973.

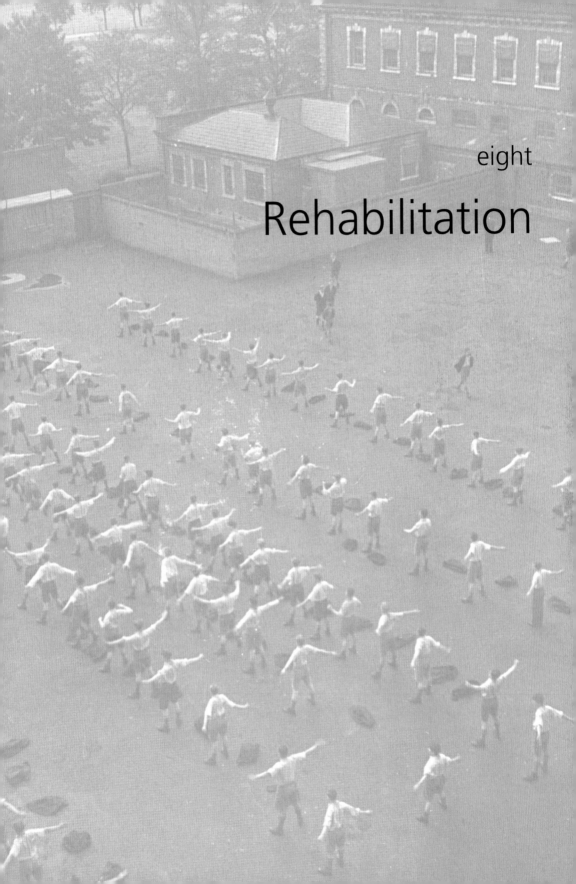

eight

Rehabilitation

Education was first formally introduced into prisons in the Parliamentary Gaol Act 1823. This stated that reading and writing must be taught in all prisons and that all prisons must have appointed schoolmasters. This photograph shows a lesson taking place in the boys' wing at HM Prison Wakefield, c. 1840. It is still a statutory condition that basic reading and writing skills must be taught to those who need it, and everyone is tested on entry to prison.

As opinion changed and it was generally accepted that prison should be more than simply retributive, the emphasis on education became more prominent. In between the wars education was provided through a small network of voluntary teachers in each prison; these mainly consisted of chaplains and borstal housemasters, with a few civilians as well. It was only after the Second World War that there was collaboration with the Department of Education and Employment, and the education system in prisons was brought up to the standard that the public receives. Here a maths class is in progress at Rochester Borstal.

In 1992 it was decided to contract out the educational services in prisons, which means that there are now a wide range of courses that can be taken, and that they are the same as the ones taught in normal schools and colleges. Inmates take courses like this science class at HM Prison The Verne, 1969, for a variety of reasons. Sometimes it is to prepare them for when they are discharged, or to keep a sense of belonging to a wider community, or sometimes it is to help pass the time whilst serving long sentences.

The fact that many prisons are sited in ageing buildings has an impact on the ability to deliver education programmes, as not all prisons have the space to cater for facilities such as this ample library at HM Prison and Borstal Institution Feltham, *c.* 1945. Modern replacements are being built but there is still plenty of room for improvement.

Prisoners who gain employment when they are discharged are much less likely to re-offend, so it is advantageous to provide opportunities to learn new skills through vocational training whilst in prison. The first vocational course introduced into prisons was precision engineering, which was introduced in 1941 at HM Prison Maidstone. Here a variety of training sessions can be seen to be going on at the same time at HM Borstal Institution Dover, 1960, including roofing, plumbing and welding.

Right: Vocational courses are taught either by specialised grades of prison officer that have previous experience in the area or by civilian instructors. Mr Barratt is the civilian instructor teaching these inmates the geometry of roofing in the carpenters' shop at HM Prison Lewes in 1971.

Below: This is a class in lettering at HM Prison Winchester, *c.* 1962. It shows an example of the wide variety of courses that are available to choose from, and prisoners are encouraged to take one whenever possible. They are important because they not only teach the skills required to do a job once released, but they also teach relevant concepts such a timekeeping and interpersonal relationships, attributes that are required in employment.

Left: Typing teacher Miss Evans and Prison Officer Fadden lead a typing lesson at HM Prison Holloway, 1977.

Below: While some gender bias did exist in courses taught in prisons, there is now a more balanced approach in modern prisons, and courses are generally available to all. This is a sewing class taking place at HM Borstal Institution East Sutton Park, 1950, an open borstal for girls.

Opposite above: A tailoring shop taught by a civilian instructor at HM Prison Blundeston, 1969.

Opposite below: A vehicle mechanics class at HM Detention Centre Latchmere House, 1966.

Above: The need for physical exercise has always been recognised by the Prison Service. Here you can see prisoners taking exercise in the yard at HM Prison Gloucester, *c.* 1900. This was done in silence, with prison warders watching carefully to prevent any attempt at communication.

Left: At the turn of the twentieth century the Medical Inspector of Prisons banned gymnastic exercise from prisons as he thought it led to suicides. Only drill exercises and formalised physical training were allowed, which, due to practical limits, was often performed in groups of up to 250. Scenes like this one at HM Prison and Borstal Institution Feltham would have been common. Only those who had a valid medical excuse were pardoned from these exercises.

The notion that gymnastics leads to suicide was revised under the new Medical Inspector of Prisons, and gymnastics classes were reinstated in the physical training of all prisoners. Here a gymnastics class is in progress at HM Prison and Borstal Institution Feltham.

Exercise has played a significant role in prisoners' reform. At HM Detention Centre Send in 1981 the 'short sharp shock' regime was followed to try to deter young offenders from re-offending. In the induction period the boys were made to run five laps, which was increased to seven laps, and for the week before they were to be released they were made to run ten laps, all of which must be done within a set time.

Above: At HM Prison and Borstal Institution Feltham the inmates are encouraged to play inter-house football. Achieving something in sport can make inmates feel they have not been wasting their time during their sentence, and gives them something to aim for.

Opposite: Young prisoners play a game of basketball at HM Prison Lewes. Sport, especially team games, can give inmates a sense of camaraderie. This is important as they are away from their family and friends, and feelings of loneliness can often prevail.

The facilities at the different institutes vary widely. At HM Borstal Institution Dover, 1964, the boys get to go canoeing in Dover harbour. Not all prisons have this geographical advantage; some of the older prisons do not even have room for a gymnasium.

There are lots of opportunities for prisoners to participate in art and craft activities in their recreation time. These include painting and drawing, carpentry, and playing musical instruments. Here inmates from HM Prison Leyhill take part in a carpentry class in 1946. The tuition fees are paid from the education budget, but the inmates have to pay for the materials they use.

Above: An art class in progress at HM Prison Maidstone. The projects undertaken in art and craft classes can also help to maintain relationships with the inmate's family, as the finished products can be given as personal presents.

Right: At HM Prison Wakefield the prisoner's artwork is put on display in the central hall. Although not all prisoners are able to produce work to such a high standard, it is generally agreed that art and craft activities are immensely beneficial. The process of carrying out the individual projects is therapeutic, satisfying and builds self-esteem.

Left: In 1962 Arthur Koestler set up the Koestler Awards to recognise exceptional talent of people in custody in the areas of art, music and literature. In 1969 these awards were extended to include industry and vocational training, and in 1973 to include live music. Every year there is a public exhibition and cash priszs are awarded to the winners. This is the 1967 exhibition, held at the Reed Paper Showrooms.

Below: At HM Prison Falfield the inmates are practicing with their band, 1960. They do this under the supervision of prison staff. Sometimes artists or theatre groups will come in to teach the inmates.

Here the inmates at HM Prison Holloway practice for a concert, to be held for the other inmates in their recreation time, *c.* 1950.

Left: HM Prison Leyhill in 1946 showing a wall newspaper called *New Dawn*. Both staff and prisoners contributed to this, and it was considered to be a privilege to have work included.

Below: Another common privilege for inmates is being allowed to have their own allotment space. Due to restrictions in the amount of available space, not many inmates can have their own plot. Here some prisoners are tending the plots at HM Prison Maidstone, 1969.

Television allows a link to what is happening outside of prison. At HM Prison Blundeston, 1969, the inmates gather together in the television room to watch a programme, though in many prisons inmates now have their own television in their cell.

Above: Before television was a popular medium, prisoners would gather in common rooms like this one at HM Prison Sudbury, *c.* 1955. It was used for writing letters and reading, and gramophone concerts would be held on an evening.

Opposite above: At HM Prison Brixton, 1972, inmates play chess in their cell.

Opposite below: An inmate plays snooker on 'D' wing at HM Prison Dartmoor, 1972.

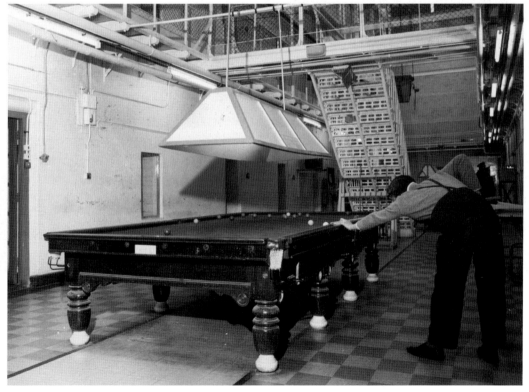

Above: Another domestic training course at HM Prison Holloway, 1964. Here, female inmates are taught how to budget for their family upon release. Courses are now not so gender biased and focus on the general issues of communication, managing relationships and life skills. The two main pre-release courses run in prisons nowadays are the Pre-release Employment Scheme and Social Work in Prison schemes, which are run by the Probation Service.

Opposite above: The first major provision for the readjustment of prisoners due to be released was the introduction of Prison Welfare Officers in 1955. These became part of the Probation Service in 1965. The concept of being released early on a licence, or parole as it is commonly known, was introduced in 1968. This is a domestic training class for mothers in HM Prison Holloway who have previously neglected their children, 1962.

Opposite below: A lecture on after-care at HM Borstal Institution Wellingborough, 1964. For the majority of prisoners after-care is not compulsory, although many take up this opportunity. It is compulsory, however, for those offenders who were under twenty-one when they were sentenced, for persistent offenders, and for those released on parole from a life sentence.

Other local titles published by Tempus

Murder & Crime: Dover

JANET CAMERON

Those who fell foul of the law in Kent faced a horrible fate: some were thrown to their deaths from the top of Dover's iconic white cliffs, whilst others were hanged, quartered, burnt or buried alive, yet still the criminal fraternity of Kent went undeterred. With more than 50 illustrations, this chilling catalogue of murderous misdeeds is bound to captivate anyone interested in the criminal history of the area.

0-7524-3978-2

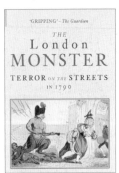

Madmen: A Social History of Madhouses, Mad-Doctors & Lunatics

ROY PORTER

Best-selling popular historian Roy Porter looks at the bizarre and savage practices of doctors for treating those afflicted by 'manias', ranging from huge doses of opium, blood-letting and cold water immersion to beatings, confinement in cages and blistering. The author also reveals how Bethlem – the London asylum created to care for the mentally sick of the capital – was riddled with sadism and embezzlement, and if that wasn't dehumanizing enough, jeering, ogling sightseers were permitted entry – for a fee of course.

0-7524-3730-5

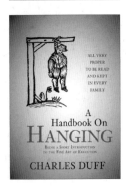

The London Monster: Terror on the Streets in 1790

JAN BONDESON

Between 1788 and 1790 a bizarre serial attacker known as the London Monster assaulted more than 50 women in the capital. During his two-year reign of terror the London Monster became a psychopathic celebrity, both celebrated and condemned in plays, newspapers and caricatures. The story has remarkable parallels to our time: a police force unable to find its man, a tabloid frenzy, and a need to convict someone at all costs, even if the evidence was questionable…

0-7524-3327-X

Handbook on Hanging

CHARLES DUFF

A Handbook on Hanging is Charles Duff's tribute to that most despised of people, the executioner, and his 'art'. In his treatise on judicial killing, Duff writes with deceptive levity about botched executions, innocent victims and a legal system that demands retribution. The result is a stunning satire on capital punishment, a polemic that reveals the hypocrisy and self-delusion inherent in a society that demands 'an eye for an eye', yet strives to make state-sponsored killing humane.

1-84588-141-9

If you are interested in purchasing other books published by Tempus, or in case you have difficulty finding any Tempus books in your local bookshop, you can also place orders directly through our website

www.tempus-publishing.com